LEARNING THE DRAGON

The Secrets of Success in College and Beyond

JACK N. COLE, Ph.D. and
TODD KENREICH, Ph.D.

Published in the United States by SchoolRubric, Inc.
Orlando, Florida

Copyright © 2024 Jack N. Cole and Todd Kenreich

All rights reserved.

Cover Design by Casey Kenreich

ISBN: 978-1-962765-99-2

TABLE OF CONTENTS

INTRODUCTION	1
CHAPTER 1 GETTING STARTED: TIME MANAGEMENT, SETTING PRIORITIES, AND ORGANIZATIONAL SKILLS TO SLAY DISTRACTIONS	6
CHAPTER 2 MASTERING THE CLASS: STUDY SKILLS REIMAGINED	37
CHAPTER 3 SOARING WITH THE ENHANCED DAVINCI NOTETAKING SYSTEM©	71
CHAPTER 4 DEVOURING THE TEXTBOOK	85
CHAPTER 5 BEFORE YOU GET STARTED ONLINE	95

CHAPTER 6   117
ASKING FOR HELP: PROBLEM
SOLVING AND NAVIGATING
BUREAUCRACY

CHAPTER 7   125
BUILDING POSITIVE
RELATIONSHIPS WITH
PROFESSORS AND PEERS

CHAPTER 8   135
GETTING READY FOR
WHAT'S NEXT

EPILOGUE   155

APPENDIX   157

ACKNOWLEDGMENTS   184

ABOUT THE AUTHORS   186

For Lynn, Jack IV, and Meredith -JNC

For Amy, Casey, Clara, and Marianne -TWK

INTRODUCTION

Each year, nearly four million students head to college in the United States, but why do some students sail to the top of the class while others drift along in the middle? How is it that success comes easily for some and not for others? It's time for you to uncover the hidden secrets of success in college. Drawing on recent developments in the science of learning, this book will provide you with a new dynamic set of tools for success in the classroom and beyond. With valuable input from more than 500 college students, we illustrate how the path to a brighter future begins with re-learning *how* to learn.

We are professors of education, and our professional work focuses on the science of learning and the art of teaching in order to build the next generation of innovative teachers. Together we have taught more than 2000 students at Towson University in Maryland, and along the way, we've learned a lot about how our students learn best. We call this the Dragon Mindset, and we want to share it with you.

Dragons are always curious about the world and how it works. They are open to new ideas, and hungry to learn more. They focus on their priorities for the short term and long term.

Dragons understand that they can't do it all on their own. They build meaningful relationships with others, and they don't hesitate to ask for help. As a result, Dragons swiftly solve problems, rebound from failure, and never give up. That's the Dragon Mindset.

We want you to be a Dragon. Borrowing from Chinese culture, we view the Dragon as a positive symbol of strength, prosperity, and good fortune. Not a hot-headed, fire-breathing beast, but a calm, cool, and confident creature. Let this symbol inspire you, and together we will help you cultivate the Dragon Mindset.

You are part of the most overscheduled generation in history, so it makes sense to begin this book with some key ideas about time management and goal setting. In Chapter 1, **"Getting Started: Time Management, Setting Priorities, and Organizational Skills to Slay Distractions,"** you'll explore how to rise above the many distractions and temptations to procrastinate. Using simple tools, you can identify your top priorities and begin to pattern your days, weeks, and months accordingly. Following a few steps, you can practice and master reliable techniques for better time management and organization.

Chapter 2 is titled **"Mastering the Class: Study Skills Reimagined,"** and in it you will learn about the Information Environment (IE), its characteristics, and how to take advantage of them to ease your progress through learning and life. You'll discover effective methods for more active listening, boosting memorization skills, and mastering your Information Environment. These study skills provide a solid foundation for test-taking skills as well. In Chapter 3, **"Soaring with the Enhanced DaVinci Notetaking System©,"** you'll apply this proven approach to your Information Environment. Chapter 4, **"Devouring the Textbook,"** introduces multiple strategies that will transform your learning. Here we highlight the vital importance of varied reading skills so that you get the highest return from your time invested with textbooks.

Chapter 5, "**Before You Get Started Online,**" reminds you that there is much more to virtual learning than meets the eye. We make the case for double-checking your technology and practicing key technology tools so that you can make a positive impression with your professors. We shift your perspective to consider how even the smallest details of your participation in live or asynchronous learning can signal to the professor whether or not you are serious about your success.

One of the fundamental problems for many students is reluctance or even shame when asking for help. In Chapter 6, "**Asking for Help: Problem Solving and Navigating Bureaucracy,**" we do our best to reframe asking for help as a natural strategy for success. This begins with asking for help during a professor's office hours. After all, professors are paid to sit in their office and be ready for student questions. Why not stop by? We include four vignettes of students who faced and overcame challenges by navigating bureaucracy. Finally, we close by reminding you of the wide range of support resources available on and off campus.

Chapter 7 is titled, "**Building Relationships with Professors and Peers,**" and in it we examine the fundamental need for building healthy relationships as a member of a college community. Students like you with ambition often need to shift from a transactional to a relational view of the world. Not only is a relational view more effective for long-term success but also this view is great for developing a stronger sense of identity and belonging. These healthy relationships can sustain you - especially when bumps and detours arise on the road to success. Next, you'll learn how (and how not to) correspond via email with professors. Professional communication requires attention to appropriate timing, polite greeting, use of proof-read sentences, and tones of civility rather than desperation or aggression. Also, we remind you that there is no need to impress every single professor in college. Instead, we urge you to cultivate stronger connections with at least two professors - preferably ones who are willing to provide a solid recommendation letter for the future. Next, we make the case for the importance of seeking out a mentor. This may be a peer who is one or two semesters closer to graduation, an alum, or a professor. We offer key considerations to help you select wisely when identifying your mentor.

In Chapter 8, "**Getting Ready for What's Next**," we begin with the premise that the path to success is far smoother when students begin college with their goals in mind. Getting ready for work, graduate school, or service means planning months or even years ahead. To facilitate this essential planning, we offer easy tools to track the specific steps needed to land a big job, apply to graduate school, or identify an important opportunity for service. While there may be a temptation for you to wait until future plans fall into place, we believe that it's never too early to get ready for what's next.

Chapters 1-8 focus on succinct advice and practical tools for success. In the Epilogue, though, we reach beyond conventional measures of success to take up one of the great, enduring questions: how to lead a good life. Drawing on our expertise in ethics, we'll share a brief discussion of the "good life" in relation to one's purpose and happiness as a compelling way to conclude this book on success.

For now, what you really want to know is how to succeed at learning in this ever-changing world of ours. The bigger and more complicated things get, the more important it is for you to control your own fate. With this in mind, a great deal of learning will occur in small and large group settings, in and outside of the classroom. You'll need to know how to organize to learn the most useful information you possibly can. This book is about how to learn in the most successful and efficient ways possible.

INTRODUCTION

It is about learning in today's sometimes confusing information environments, whatever and wherever they are.

In brief, this book will teach you how to learn more effectively and be in greater control. You have been learning all of your life. We know that. This book, if used for your next learning, will make it faster, more effective, more enjoyable, and more beneficial to you in the long run. Invest a little time now in using these strategies for success, and you'll be repaid handsomely. Let's get started!

This is the first of a series of boxes through the book that highlight student perspectives.

"At the beginning of the semester we did an overview of everything we would complete throughout the year, and I was not looking forward to it because it seemed like a ton of work. As the semester went on, I liked how we broke each project into sections, so I could focus on and prioritize certain tasks. That forced me to look at my work from a different angle, which really opened my mind to a different way of thinking."
- Excerpt from a Second-Year Student's Course Reflection

CHAPTER 1
GETTING STARTED: TIME MANAGEMENT, SETTING PRIORITIES, AND ORGANIZATIONAL SKILLS TO SLAY DISTRACTIONS

Jack Cole

"This is your moment. Own it."
— Oprah Winfrey

We are writing this at the end of a college semester. We both teach a course in professional ethics in the Department of Secondary and Middle School Education in our College of Education. Professor Kenreich's area of focus is teaching and learning in the social studies. Professor Cole is focused on instructional arts and the science of learning.

At the time of this writing, we are in the process of finalizing grades and evaluating student work. Since endings often mark

GETTING STARTED: SKILLS TO SLAY DISTRACTIONS

new beginnings, we have some news for those in college or getting ready for it: control of your time is the first real key to success. For our courses, those students who have respected their time – and ours – have fared the best in the quest for success and high grades. Those who have not, have not done well in our courses.

> One of our best learners had this to say about her new strategies for success:
>
> "One of the most important things that I learned from this semester is the importance of using a calendar and using the calendar correctly. Before taking this class, I didn't have a good system of organizing my assignments and other things I needed to do. However, this course introduced me to using a calendar system where I list every assignment due date for the whole semester. Also I schedule when I have to start doing things and when I have to have things done by in order to have time to polish it. Then, I list the resources needed in order to complete these assignments. In all honesty, at first, I was not really thrilled with the idea of having to do the calendar for the whole semester. However, as the semester progressed, the calendar played one of the most important roles for me to succeed in this class. It helped me keep track of things without procrastinating or forgetting assignments.
>
> Going forward, I will use this calendar in my future semesters, and even after college when I have a career. In fact, I was inspired by the calendar for this class to use a similar calendar for my other classes this semester. I can say that it helped me keep on top of things without stressing out or hurrying to do things at the last minute. I will always use this calendar system for my future semesters and also for my future career so that I may always be on top of things." -First-Year Student

The information in this chapter is for you – if you wish to manage your learning over time. If you extend your calendar into the future, you have better control over the course of your life. It will give you more control because it allows you to develop a strategy for working. It also encourages you to attain a broader idea of what you do, your purpose, and what the achievement of each task means to you in terms of your overall education.

The purpose of what follows is to put you in charge of your learning, with your professor, books, classmates and resources as tools for you to use in doing that. Many learners do not do this – instead, they put one foot ahead of another – and end up with an education that is a loose collection of mostly unconnected ideas. This is not a worthy return on the investment that you make. It is better to have an integrated outlook on life and learning – and on how you get that done.

The Dragons say, "Procrastinate tomorrow." Let us explain. We all have much to do. We have 168 hours a week to accomplish our tasks. This includes sleep, work, recreation, exercise, eating, going places and everything else. Time is our most precious resource. How we spend time determines how well we do. If we spend it well, we generally do well; if we do not, we generally do not do well. There is no magic, perhaps, except for how we organize ourselves to use our time. There's real magic there.

You can work that magic with your time if you follow a few simple rules. Yes, it's work – but work done now saves you much work and rework later. So, consider this the first day of your academic career. Here's how to start managing your time right now. Forget everything you think you know about the subject. It may have gotten you to where you are now, but you need to go beyond it. So clear your mind.

We will begin by dealing with everything we need to do. Nothing else. That will come later. We will select one course of study and nail things down for it. Then we'll add more. If you follow these steps, you will be successful. Once you've got things laid out, all you'll need is persistence to succeed. Persistence is the one personal quality that contributes the most to success. There are no shortcuts. (That's a big secret.)

> "In college, your life isn't as structured as it was in high school, so it's on you to create a structure for yourself that makes you successful." -Second-Year Student

First, get yourself a blank monthly calendar. You will need five pages to manage time over a semester. They will get messy. That's OK, since life is messy. We like the blank calendar that Microsoft Word will generate for you. Use landscape mode, to make it easy. Print them out now.

Once you have your calendar page, put in the month and year at the top and number the days in the boxes. Sometimes you need to add a date box at the bottom. Go ahead. You're a learner. You can do it.

The next step is to strategize your time. As a reminder, you have 168 hours a week (7 days a week times 24 hours a day) – no more and no less. During this time, you must eat, sleep, work, commute, and do all of your activities. Planful allocation of time will help you do this. Follow the steps below to complete the first version of your calendar. You'll be updating it constantly while you use it. Use a pencil or use a pen. A pencil is better. You'll see. Things change.

Step 1: Gather all of the information you have about the course. You want to find what nearly all courses call "Due Dates." It is essential that your teacher or professor list these at the beginning of the semester. You can even email, write, and text or call your professor to get this information before the semester. Smart students do this. Even a rough idea is good enough to start.

If you can't get these in advance, start this step at the beginning of the semester when the professor announces them or gives you a syllabus. If you get a professor who won't or can't give these to you, consider switching sections. The prospects for the course being worthwhile aren't very good. Of course, there are circumstances that indicate otherwise, but the odds are stacked against you.

Now that you have your list of Due Dates, write them on your calendar. For the entire semester. You may want to use red pencils for this, so that the dates stand out. This is a good start. By the way, that's usually all that most people do. It makes life difficult for them, but you're being enlightened, so onward we go.

Step 2: Imagine this: there are days when we will not be doing any schoolwork at all. These are called "Down Dates," and this is important: identify these days in advance and you'll be able to honor them. Be as specific as you can. Get them on the calendar by drawing an "X" on the day you decide is going to be a Down Date. Candidates for this special indication include birthdays, getting married (or attending a wedding), planned trips, days of recognition (Super Bowl Sunday, St. Patrick's Day, Easter, Juneteenth, Fourth of July, Eid al-Adha, Yom Kippur and personal obligation days), etc. For each of these days, or half-day, place an "X" on your calendar – and perhaps use a special color for these. You can always cancel them, but knowing what's coming up on your calendar will make it better for you in planning your time. You need to block these days out on your calendar – but you rarely need to explain them. Just say "I have personal business that day." Most people respect that.

Step 3: Ask yourself how far in advance of the Due Date you should begin work on each "deliverable." Deliverables are assignments you submit for evaluation. They may be final or intermediate work or a test, but each should have its Due Date already on the calendar. Here's a hint that leads to success: Estimate how much Lead Time you should allow for each assignment. That allows you to estimate a Start Date for each assignment. This practice is a procrastination buster (yeah, "procrastinate tomorrow" is our motto here). It's far better to make a start when you have identified a good starting date than it is to keep putting work off and being strapped for time near the Due Date. If you know that you have a tendency to procrastinate, extend some grace to yourself and plan your time accordingly (Wohl et al., 2010). Below, you will find an example of a chart developed for a typical semester.

Assignment	Time to Complete	Due Date	Start Date
Research Paper	4 weeks	Oct. 15	Sept. 15
Reading Report	3 days	Nov. 15	Nov. 12
Project	4 weeks	Nov. 30	Oct. 30
Exam Study	1 week	Dec. 1	Nov. 25
Final Exam	All semester	Last class	Second week of semester
Special Presentation	3 weeks	Oct. 25	Oct. 1

The example gives you a way to stretch your work out so that you aren't trying to do any task all at once. *Work –break – return to work – break – return* again gives you the best chance for producing a truly fine deliverable. This is usually how it's done on the job with projects that are not assigned at the last minute – doing the work a little at a time, balancing responsibilities, and fitting things together near the end time generally produces a successful product.

Actually, the example above oversimplifies things. Not by much, but by enough to mean that success is not assured. We need to do one thing more: granularize things. This means that you break your assignments into the steps needed to complete them.

Step 4. Task Analysis. For each deliverable, you should break it into steps – working backwards from submitting it. This gives you a fresh way of looking at things and will result in you skipping useless work that you have learned to do by force of habit. You will be amazed by seeing all the steps you complete in preparing your deliverables! You will also see which ones may be done at the same time, since they are highly related to each other. Examples may be seen below – but these are examples, and your style of working may be different. Feel free to edit these according to the assignment and how you work. Each step gets a calendar date.

GETTING STARTED: SKILLS TO SLAY DISTRACTIONS

April 2023

Sunday	Monday	Tuesday	Wednesday	Thursday	Friday	Saturday
						1 Do Case Pt. 5
2 Down	3 Did: Case Pt. 5	4 Due: Case Part 5	5	6	7 Start Case Pt. 5	8
9 Down	10 Start/Do: Reading 7	11 Do: Reading 7	12 Do/Did: Reading 7	13 Due: Reading 7	14 Down	15
16 Down	17	18 Start/Do: Notes 4 (polish and get ready for submission)	19 Did: (Submit) Notes 4	20 Due: Notes 4	21	22
23 Down	24 Start/Do: LGBTX? Report	25 Do: LGBTX? Report	26 Did: LGBTX? Report	27 Due: LGBTX? Report	28	29
30 Down						

Resources: Wifi, Laptop, Coffee, More Coffee, A quiet space, Ethics textbook

February

Resources
- iPad
- Notebook
- Stationary
- Textbook
- Google

SUNDAY	MONDAY	TUESDAY	WEDNESDAY	THURSDAY	FRIDAY	SATURDAY
			1	2 Learner Survey	3	4
5 Calendar	6 Notes Calendar	7	8 Calendar Notes 1 Reading 1	9 Reading 1	10 Reading 2	11
12 Reading 1, Reading 2	13 Reading 2	14 Reading 2, Reading 2		15 Reading 2, Case pt 2	16	17 Case pt 1	18
19 Case pt 2, Reading 3	20 Reading 3	21 Case pt 1, Reading 3	22 Topic 12	23 Reading 3, Topic 12, Reading 4	24 Case pt 2, Topic 12	25 Case pt 2, Reading 4
26 Case pt 5, Case pt 12, Topic 12	27 Case pt 3, Reading 4	28 Case pt 3, Topic Presentation				

Color Key
- Due — Do
- Down — Did

Example: Research Paper

If you do these steps well, your work will appear to have been effortless on your part. That speaks volumes. But you must invest the necessary time. Note: we're working backwards here. For some reason, this seems to help to prevent omitting necessary steps. When you are done reading this list, read it again in reverse (starting with number 13 and ending with 1).

GETTING STARTED: SKILLS TO SLAY DISTRACTIONS

1. <u>Submission of Paper.</u> (Due Date or before) Really good learners often turn things in a little early. This allows them to get good commentary back and demonstrates a good work ethic. This is worth a great deal.

2. <u>Last-Minute Scan of Paper.</u> It is on the way to turn work into the instructor that one often sees the most glaring errors. (I once took 100 resumes to a conference only to find that "Address" was misspelled with only one *d*. They all went into the trash. This is like applying for a job at a school and misspelling the word "principal" on the cover letter. Into the trash goes your application.) You should plan to scan for typos and other errors and to correct them before submission.

3. <u>Final Proofreading, Spell Check and Correction.</u> "Fit and finish" refers to how a document looks to the reader. Misspellings, poor punctuation and incorrect words catch the reader's eye and often get in the way of understanding and accepting ideas. It is critical that you give what you've written a final "polishing," both in terms of meaning and expression – and in terms of the details that strike the reader's eye. This contributes a great deal to the credibility of the work and puts the reader at ease and more likely to agree with your thinking. Also, looks count!

4. <u>Converting Rough Draft into Final Draft.</u> Look at your work from front to back – and again from back to front. Read it with a ruler, line by line. Get a true friend to work with you. Your friend will see errors that you do not – and a true friend will tell you. Don't forget to thank your friend.

5. <u>Trimming Useless Text from Your Final Draft.</u> If you have insufficient research or have little to say about some of the topics in your outline, pitch them. They won't be missed. Just re-read your work to see if it has the continuity that you desire it to have.

6. <u>Finalize Your Notes and Outline into a Final Draft.</u> This is the step that many people call "writing the paper," but there is more involved in producing a worthy paper than just slamming words into an outline. But it's a needed start.

7. <u>Research the Topics on Your Rough Outline.</u> Read articles, books, online postings and other information, the results of database searches, interview knowledgeable individuals, speak to a research librarian, or perhaps go to the writing center near you for a review. Take good notes, and especially note the information you will need for citations and references to substantiate your research. **This should take you at least 3 sessions, spread over time, and possibly more.** The pros spend a good amount of time on this. Amateurs, not so much. It is where you gather the wisdom that you will include in your paper.

8. <u>Make a List of Possible Sources to Research.</u> These include online sources, library sources, research librarians, publications and books. Spend some time assembling this and gathering information. Phone some libraries and ask to whom you should talk. Then call them. This is to be the basis of your paper, so do not skimp on this.

9. <u>Turn your Rough Outline into a Series of Questions.</u> These questions will be addressed and answered through your research.

10. <u>Write a Series of Section Headings</u> for your paper or list questions that you will answer. These should show the building of an argument or discussion exploring and answering your key question.

11. <u>Turn your Selected Topics into a Broad Question to be Explored, Explained, and Defended.</u> This question frames the course of your entire work and suggests ideas to consider in the process of answering it. If you were to break your question

apart, idea by idea, into its components, you could turn them into possible headings, or general descriptions, of portions of your question. Then you could assemble sources from books, podcasts, articles, speeches and other sources to back each one up, support it, give information about it or let the reader know that you share the opinions of others.

12. <u>Select the Topic for your Paper.</u> What's it to be about? What area will it explore? Can you learn more than you know now by exploring it? Use the list of suggested topics provided by your professor. Conduct an Internet search. Start with Google Scholar or ChatGPT. Explore the key databases of your college library or contact a librarian. Select something you have an interest in exploring. If you can't find a topic of interest, find out what your professor considers to be interesting. Perhaps ask a professional in the field. This is an important step, since it determines everything else you will do. Perhaps give yourself 3 days to list several topics and to explore before your final selection. Once you have selected the topic, commit to it and to doing a good job of exploring it.

13. <u>Put the Due Date for your paper onto your calendar.</u> Then you will add dates for intermediate steps. (See above.) Perhaps color code each step. Do this as you figure out how much lead time to give each subtask.

> "I love that Professor Cole [had us] make calendars with all assignments and due dates/deadlines because this is what really helped me stay on track throughout the semester."
> - Second-Year Student

Experts in project management offer the insight that the ratio of planning time to doing time should be 80/20. They also tell us that no one ever gets this much time, so collapsing planning time into ongoing doing time is about the best we can do. The steps above reflect this insight. By carefully allocating our time and collapsing steps as necessary, we increase our chances of doing a good job. Working backwards during the planning step allows you to save time and trouble as you proceed. Professionals tell us that fixing a problem at the beginning of a project usually only costs 10% of what it would take to fix it when the project is further along. See the example below to see how backwards planning can help with smoother preparation and better outcomes. The pros use this strategy. So can you.

Example: Reading Report (may be edited/adapted for Lab and other reports)

1. **Submit final written report.**

2. **Review final written report just before submission** – spell check, grammar check, proofread. If you can, have a friend look it over.

3. **Convert final notes and headings into final report draft.**

4. **Review notes and determine if you need to revise, add or delete headings.**

5. **Read thoroughly and take notes for headings you will use.**

6. **Establish needed headings for your report.** Typically, your instructor will give you these. If not, base them on the sections in the chapter. Include an opening and a closing.

7. **Review the chapter on which you will report.** Survey the chapter from beginning to end, taking note of headings. If there are no headings visible (boldface items, for instance), create your own and record them. Look at headings, pictures, italicized or boldfaced

words and terms. Do not read the chapter – overview it and take notes.

8. **Assemble your needed materials** – book/chapter, computer/printer, paper, and other needed items. You would be surprised at how many people neglect this and have to scramble later. Running out of paper, ink and other items late at night is a serious inconvenience.

   Also, do not order the book online and find yourself waiting weeks to get a copy of a book to save $2. Get the book early on and pay what you need to in order to have it in a timely fashion. You probably should have your own copy. Sharing a book is a recipe for disaster (just like loaning your notes raises the possibility of them being in Argentina the night before the final --- that has happened.)

9. **Get the assignment from your instructor, web site, course calendar in the syllabus, or instructor.** Get all of the particulars and store them where you can retrieve them. It makes sense to store them in a subdirectory on your computer (and not in the "cloud," which is a place from which you can be cut off at the most inopportune moment). Why not just trust a classmate? You do so at your peril.

10. **Put the Due Date on your calendar.** Fill in the rest of the intermediate dates to allow room for you to successfully complete the assignment.

11. **Read the specifications for the assignment.** What are the requirements? Length? Font, font size, spacing, paging, inclusion of name and dates, page numbers? Will the chapter assignments all follow the same pattern? In this case, set up a template to save yourself time and make copies for each chapter you must read.

Example: Project

Completing a project is pretty much the same as writing a research paper, with perhaps more active investigation required. However, doing a group project is different, since others are involved in getting it done. Planning of steps and due dates must be done with several people involved. (Hint: most people today use a conferencing program online for holding meetings, which are much easier to schedule this way.) Success here requires keeping track of more variables.

It also requires close interaction with group members from beginning to end. And it requires attention to managing the steps (and people) involved in successful completion all along the way. Most teachers and professors do not fully appreciate all of the moving parts involved in the successful completion of group work. This being the case, group members' best recourse is to take charge of the project themselves and plan and implement steps in a fashion that includes a strong management component of the work. In order to do this, they need knowledge of the parts involved and a commitment of group members to make certain that those parts work harmoniously together. If they have this knowledge and commitment, group members can function as a self-directed work team (SDWT) – an entity much prized by managers, but often sorely lacking in practice.

Have you ever been a member of a group tasked with doing a project? It is very common to encounter the following problems:

1. Not all group members have the same level of commitment to the project
2. The group has no norms of behavior and contribution governing individuals' activities

3. No one manages the timeline, so contributions are uncoordinated
4. There are not enough members in the group to sustain the work
5. Group members do not have assigned roles, nor are they held to their timely completion
6. No one manages the conscious attention to the business of the group
7. Some members do very little work at all, seemingly preferring to ride the coattails of those doing the work
8. Some members do more than their fair share
9. Some members disappear and do not complete their tasks
10. Some members do not get along with other members
11. All members of assigned group work receive the same grade, so the good workers are pulled down by the lassitude of the "loafers"

Ponder these points carefully. They all affect your learning. They all affect your GPA. They all diminish the value or the return on your investment (dollars and time and effort) in your education. They are all subject to being able to be controlled through proper action.

In order to function effectively, groups should have seven or more members. Groups below this threshold subject themselves to stress and to a higher chance of failure. At the very least, they are open to one or two people doing all of the work. Instructors don't realize this, so they tend to set up groups of 5 learners – and everyone pays the price for this. Projects are completed, perhaps, but first-rate work is rare. Group members have less of an idea about what they are doing and why their individual contribution is important. Groups that "fly blind" in this way produce work of lower quality, and committed members develop a distaste for group work at all. Groups that just "fall into place" and work well together are few.

I do not assign group work without teaching my learners how to function in a group and how to manage their own learning.

I also set up a ground rule for my groups (and I think it should also apply in business): a simple majority vote of any group can cast any member out. That member needs to find a way into another group, or a way back into the good graces of their first group or suffer the consequence of needing to do an entire project solo. This is tough, but it seems to work.

Although the ultimate success of all learners is one of my responsibilities, I know that the freedom to fail is a first step in achieving ultimate success. One person's exercise of free will should never be allowed to inflict damage on peers, colleagues or classmates.

To achieve success, a group needs a task, a timeline, management and coordination of work, enough time to complete the task successfully and sufficient members to make for equitable distribution of work. If these things are present, all group members have a dual-level successful experience: their work will be of high quality, and their learnership will be enhanced and molded through the experience of working with others.

Example: Exam Study

This ought to be a snap. Smart learners space out their exam prep. Others wait until the last minute and then cram. Cramming may work for some, but research supports the notion that the information "crammed" is lost soon after the exam.

Consider this: perhaps you take 5 courses. Perhaps you pay $7000 in tuition. That means each course costs you $1400. Suppose that there are 43 sessions in the semester. Many folks miss 3 or so. That means that each of the 40 sessions represents an investment (in your education) of 1400/40, or $35.

GETTING STARTED: SKILLS TO SLAY DISTRACTIONS

And this is just the tuition for one course session – not counting fees, board, transportation and other expenses, which certainly factor in.

Each session presents you with information, either spoken, shown, encased in written material or otherwise made available to you. This represents the universe of knowledge that teachers sample in the preparation of an exam. Sometimes this is done by random selection and sometimes it is done by selecting the most important information. Most of us who teach do a combination of these. Knowledge of important items is something we value, and this lets us know who has mastered that. Knowledge of randomly selected information tells us about your depth of knowledge. You should always expect both.

Unfortunately, capturing this information is not particularly easy, unless you use a notetaking system like the one below – the Enhanced DaVinci Notetaking System©. Its features allow for easy capture of details and ideas and for separating out the most important ones. We will share much more about this in Chapter 3.

Preparing for an examination successfully involves time management. By following these steps, you have increased the probability that you will be the most prepared for the exam that you can be.

Follow these steps (backwards, of course):

1. Get the results of the test and see where you need to improve
2. Take the exam
3. Perform a grand review the day or evening before the exam and then get 8 hours of sleep
4. Review all the information you have learned up until each intermediate date; self-testing in the announced format usually produces the best results

5. Establish 5-6 intermediate review dates between the start and the exam and calendar those
6. Establish a date (3 or 4 weeks) in advance of the exam and put that on your calendar
7. Gather and organize the materials of yours that contain the information you'll need – including URLs
8. Find out what the exam will cover and what its format will be
9. Put the exam date and time in your calendar
10. Find out the date of your exam as soon as you can

Example: Final Exam

Final exams look at learning over a whole semester's time or they look at what you've learned since the last exam. If the latter, see above. In fact, you'd be smart to plan cumulative study for your final as you encounter each exam in the semester.

The steps for the final are the same as those for a regular exam. At the time of the final, many learners have the semester's grade or a P/F in the balance. Finals require special attention.

So, in addition to scheduling your time in the same way as you do for a regular exam, do the following (again, in reverse order):

1. Examine the results of your final exam and plan for the future
2. Take the exam
3. Get 8 hours' sleep the night before.
4. Have a high-intensity study session the night before your final
5. Conduct planned and spaced study sessions, with a small group of (serious) classmates if possible
6. Establish a schedule for study geared to the final
7. Gather all materials you could possibly find that relate to information you will need

8. Find out the format of the final and what it will cover – how much of your final grade it represents
9. Write the date of the final exam in your calendar

Example: Presentations

Presentation work follows the same basic guidelines as does that of Project work. In this case, usually one or two people are tasked with presenting information or a topic. Presenters need to organize their time to make room for the following activities. Again, the activities are to begin at the bottom of the list and culminate in the presentation and post-evaluation at the top. Intermediate work and due dates are critical to the success of a presentation, considering that a rehearsal step is necessary toward the end of the process. Development of a presentation that does not include rehearsal for knowledgeability and fluency is basically a waste of time.

The steps of doing a good presentation are (last to first):

1. Get feedback on how presentation went
2. Deliver presentation, using a clock or timer
3. Dress for success, including the background against which you will present
4. Final assembly of script and delivery tools
5. Test the equipment you will use. If you do not, it will betray you every time
6. Rehearse, Rehearse, Rehearse – for timing, emphases, flow
7. Finalize script and order of presentation slides, timing, and emphasized delivery
8. Learn all words so that you can pronounce them fluidly and flawlessly
9. Develop presentation slides to accompany your presentation outline
10. Based on your research/notes, develop an outline for your presentation

11. Assemble and research information for your presentation
12. Locate needed sources of information
13. Develop preliminary outline for your presentation
14. Clarify specifics of presentation – delivery date, length, format, rubric for evaluation, suggested sources
15. Receive or decide on the topic for presentation

Doing good presentations is an art as well as a science. The same steps that guide good group/individual projects apply here. There is also a good dose of manners and civility included in the mix. You are giving a gift to your audience. Your audience is giving you the gift of their attention and an opportunity to communicate with them. Respect your audience.

The more presentations you give, the better you will get. People enjoy good presentations. They suffer through or disengage from poor ones. You want your presentations to be appreciated and sought after.

Sample Task Analysis Plan for Typical Semester's Work

Earlier in this chapter, we discussed an example for breaking work down as you plan a semester. Looking at your calendar, assign each task a Due (submission) date, a Start (Do) Date, a Finish-By (Done) date – and enough time between each of these to allow for "life to happen."

This format allows you to disassemble each assignment. Once you have done your date-assignments (in pencil is a good idea), transfer them to your monthly calendar coded as Start, Done and Finish dates, along with the resources you will need to complete them. Each of these is a calendar entry – Start, Done and Finish. Our recommendation is that you use an Excel (or other) spreadsheet to do this. This will make changes much easier. If you use an advanced formula and use date-additive formulas, changes will ripple.

GETTING STARTED: SKILLS TO SLAY DISTRACTIONS

Setting Priorities

School is a time for sorting things out and establishing priorities. We set long-term priorities. We set intermediate-term priorities. We set day to day priorities. Doing these things effectively makes us progress throughout life and generally achieve success.

There are many books available to you regarding this. Now what we will do is to give you some guidelines and practices useful to you as you select and sort your own priorities. We like brainstorming, so we'll use a process called *mind-mapping* (others have called this process other things, such as *concept mapping)* and use a computer program such as Inspiration© to demonstrate it. This process lets you keep many things in mind at one time without losing high-quality ideas through being overloaded with details.

We'll start with the basics: priorities are expressions of goals. Things you want to do. Conditions you want to establish. Now, today, tomorrow, or later.

Priorities are based on your vision of a future you want to see emerge. They're not dreams. They may come from dreams. They are not objectives, although they may come from objectives. They are statements of how you want things to be – even if you have to do them yourself. In fact, that's the way most of them are met.

Consider them to be a to-do list for yourself. You can do them sequentially – one after the other – or concurrently, which is a big word for *at the same time*. Many people call this multitasking.

Research suggests that multitasking is a cruel fiction. Although humans may have 17 different and concurrent states of consciousness, only one of them is at the forefront of consciousness at any one time. Then we switch tasks, which may mean 10 seconds on one priority followed by 10 seconds on another, then back to the first. It's easy to lose priorities that way.

Anyway, you work from a list –

- Do Priority 1 to completion
- Do Priority 2 to completion

Or, work from a list that allows virtual concurrency, with forgiveness for conflicting schedules.

This could be conceived of as working your way down a table or chart, switching as one goes. Because many of the things we do involve responses from others, we need a way to put priorities on the "back burner" while we continue to move ahead on others.

GETTING STARTED: SKILLS TO SLAY DISTRACTIONS

Consider this chart that contains priorities that overlap in time.

Time	Priority 1 Grad School	Priority 2 Save and Invest	Priority 3 Live/Work in Hawaii
1	Explore Programs	Establish income source	Explore opportunities in Hawaii
2		Open savings account	Decide on course of action
3	Connect w/ Programs	Begin saving	Implement steps to getting there
4		Learn about investing	
5	Decide on Program		Move/work
6		Open investment account	
7	Apply	Continue investing	

Once you have established priorities and their sequence, transfer them to a long-term calendar that you look at daily. Also, break each priority into action items to add to the calendar which result in a successfully achieved priority. You can certainly handle multiple priorities, but careful planning and replanning can go a long way to assuring that you achieve them. Some of the boxes are empty because no task-related work occurs there.

If you don't control your time, it controls you. If you don't control your time, someone else will. The choice is yours.

1. Make a list of your priorities – work, education, love, travel, finance, health, and sports.
2. Separate them into categories.
3. For each category, identify action items.
4. Review.
5. Place these things onto a calendar; if they overlap, use color-coding.
6. Review and do each action as it comes up in the rotation; don't wait for "inspiration" to strike.

GETTING STARTED: SKILLS TO SLAY DISTRACTIONS

But you can use Inspiration to do the job, as seen below.

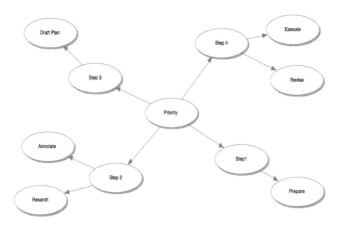

Now, each set of steps is organized around its priority statement. The order of the steps ought to be clear from the mind map above. You then break each step into smaller steps and transfer these to your calendar for each priority. Though the list can get very lengthy, keeping the steps separated in this way helps clear things up. (Inspiration© has a function key that turns the diagram into a standard outline, which is handy for double-checking sequence.)

We have provided an example of expanding the series of steps for investing, which can be directly transferred to a calendar. Organizing and sequencing this, we get an organized picture of what we have to do.

Now we transfer these steps to a calendar and, by following them, we can achieve our priority. We can also alter our priorities and our sequence of activities as needed.

This method may seem simplistic, but it has benefits:

- If you use it, it will probably work; not otherwise
- It puts you in control of your time and helps you look ahead
- It is organized into activities you have the ability to complete
- It keeps you from having to do too many things at once
- It is the key method used by professionals to organize their lives
- Plan – you get there; don't plan – where does that take you?

Yes, your calendar will change frequently. Doing it on paper makes for easy changes. Using a computer to do it often costs you more time and trouble than it is worth, especially since things ripple through time as changes need to be made. The choice is yours. Our bet is on using paper at first and then, if you must or feel that it will help, transfer to a computer. Excel or another spreadsheet will work fairly well.

The key to success is that you use this method and refer to it frequently. Making this process a weekly review is an excellent idea. Ever wonder where your friends are who are out of touch or unavailable for hanging out? They're probably planning or implementing their plan where you don't see them. They know that life is about investing time wisely. Follow their example.

Doodle can help to organize and synchronize schedules of various people. ToDoIst is one of many apps that can help you manage activities. In the end, the best app is the one that you consistently use.

GETTING STARTED: SKILLS TO SLAY DISTRACTIONS

> "If you're here, don't waste your money! You'll get as much out of college as the effort you put in. Stay organized, plan ahead, be respectful to your professors, and read the syllabus!" -First-Year Student

Handling Distractions

A distraction is an unwanted interruption in the task you are working to complete.

Sounds simple? Distractions are everywhere, all of the time. Dealing with distractions is a common topic, and to mention all of the sources of suggestions would be exhausting. Just fire up your browser and go look for "handling distractions" and you'll be swamped with possibilities. Perhaps to the point where dealing with distractions in itself becomes a distraction.

Let's embark on a voyage to look at a possible way to master all of those things that tug on, or demand, your attention. I learned it the hard way. You can, too. There's no easy way to learn it, so you may as well start now.

I'm going to show you how to handle distractions, or to avoid distractions. Distractions are features of the Information Environment. J. J. Gibson defines the Information Environment as everything around (and inside) us which perceptions can turn into meaningful items. Distractions are part of this. In fact, viewed from the proper perspective, they are the Information Environment through which we all travel. All alarms, requests, pokes, prodding are events that derail and absorb our attention are much of what the Information Environment contains.

The key element in dealing with all this is: focus on what you are doing or where you are going in the Information Environment.

Start with your current priority. Pay close attention to that. Look closely at its elements and at its current demands on you. Work through it one step at a time. Give your full attention to each step. Everything that takes you away from this is a waste of your time.

We have found that the deeper a state of concentration we are able to achieve, the easier this gets. When fully absorbed, we can attain a state of flow, which blocks out the rest of the Information Environment by requiring our full energy to deal with our priority. Time changes, sensation changes, productivity changes. You may have trouble de-coupling from your activity when you are done – or changing attention to something else when interrupted during your work. This is a state each of us can achieve (Csikszentmihalyi, 2013), and learning how to deal with this in advance can help you to preserve it.

The lines below are from one of the most exquisite poems of all time in the English language. As Samuel Taylor Coleridge was writing "Kubla Khan," someone knocked on the door, and he lost the last lines – forever. What a loss! We'd love to see the rest of the poem, but it's lost.

> In Xanadu did Kubla Khan
> A stately pleasure-dome decree:
> Where Alph, the sacred river, ran
> Through caverns measureless to man
> Down to a sunless sea.
> (Coleridge, 1816)

Have you ever lost a great idea by submitting to distraction? A great sentence for a research paper? The perfect email you were about to send? A quotation you wanted to use later? Capture, capture, capture before loss in all cases is the rule. Stay focused. Poor Coleridge! We hope this doesn't happen to you, but the odds are that it already has. Although leaving a task and returning to work on it some more is a time-honored method of moving forward, you must leave a "placeholder" so that you can take up the task again and move forward.

Practice focus. Let no one disturb you. Build Kubla Khan's dome around yourself and let everything bounce off of it. As my uncle used to say about phone calls, "Let it ring. If it's important, they can call back." Today this means turning off notifications on your phone for blocks of time so that you can stay focused.

This is the point in the chapter where we tell you to get started focusing on your priorities to block out distractions. This is where we'd say, "Record your instances of focusing success in your daily calendar." You need to decide to do it and then do it. The first step on the path of success is to celebrate your success and look forward to more.

Conclusion

With the Dragon Mindset, you can enhance your self-control and handle all that life has in store for you. Mastery of the ideas in this chapter will put you in control of your life and learning. Master these ideas one at a time and you'll have energy and productive power beyond your imagination.

References

Coleridge, S. T. (1816). *Kubla Khan.*

Csikszentmihalyi, M. (2013). *Flow: The psychology of happiness.* Random House.

Pauk, W. (2013). *How to study in college.* Cengage Learning.

Wohl, M. J. A., Pychyl, T. A., & Bennett, S. H. (2010). I forgive myself, now I can study: How self-forgiveness for procrastinating can reduce future procrastination. *Personality and Individual Differences, 48*(7), 803-808.

Further Reading

David Allen, *Getting Things Done*

> The power of Allen's popular approach lies in its multiple horizons of focus (from the immediate to long-term) that help you identify and prioritize your commitments to others and yourself. He also challenges you to envision what "wild success" would look like for you.

James Clear, *Atomic Habits*

> Clear's book helps you develop better habits with a reminder that even small adjustments to your habits can make a big difference.

Stephen Covey, *The 7 Habits of Highly Effective People*

> Covey's best-selling book invites you to write a mission statement for your life and identify your true priorities by putting "first things first."

Cal Newport, *Deep Work*

> Newport, a computer scientist, explains that multi-tasking is not as efficient as we might think. He urges everyone to set aside regular blocks of time—without distractions—for highly creative thinking that he calls deep work

CHAPTER 2
MASTERING THE CLASS:
STUDY SKILLS REIMAGINED

Jack Cole

"The secret to success is to do
the common things uncommonly well."
— John D. Rockefeller

Before we introduce essential skills and strategies for learning like a Dragon, we need to understand the Information Environment and our purposes for learning.

The Information Environment

All of us live and breathe in the Information Environment. It is composed of all of the information of which we are aware – and of all the information of which we are not. It looks like this:

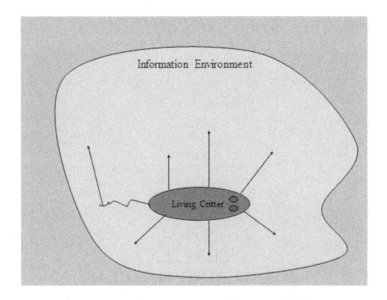

The concept is from J. J. Gibson's (1972) classic book, *The Senses Considered as Perceptual Systems*. It contains the following key ideas:

1. All living systems explore and respond to information in their environment
    a. With one-celled creatures, this is a direct interaction
    b. With multi-celled creatures, there is usually a central nervous system of some sort
2. This central nervous system receives stimuli from the outside environment
3. The entire universe consists of various realities that the central nervous system parses into information
4. Information is parsed into "percepts," which are combinations of associated cell assemblies
5. These cell assemblies represent the outside (or internal) world to the organism
6. Percepts are nonverbal representations of the stimuli perceived

7. Percepts are accompanied by conditioned reflex actions
8. If "food" is perceived, the organism moves towards it if hungry
9. If "danger" is perceived, the organism moves away
10. The organism is constantly monitoring the environment around it for opportunity and threat
11. Higher-level organizations have more highly developed central nervous systems
12. These systems sometimes acquire the use of "language," the use of "words," "phrases," "propositions" or "statements about reality" that may be combined in certain ways (syntax) to produce "meaning," or "information," upon which the organism may act (and which are themselves cell assemblies)
13. Our conscious executive function may formulate purposes or priorities, which act as influencers of decision making as we live
14. Organizations like you and I "see" reality through perceptions parsed into meaning

Current perceptual psychology and neurophysiology elaborate the increasing complexity of our collection of "parsers," which are part of "consciousness." While we may have 17 or more independent consciousnesses, we are only aware of (the "I" or executive function recognizes and uses) one at a time. Maintaining focus is one of the key components of avoiding distractions, by the way.

We are basically one with and a part of the Information Environment, in a real sense. But, there is one more key characteristic of the Information Environment. Each of us has one that is unique, and it grows and becomes more complex over time. This process never ends, thanks to our life experiences, technology and the constantly growing amount of available information.

When born, we have a small Information Environment. (This probably begins before birth, with the development of our central nervous system.)

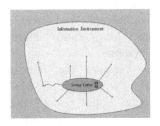

Light	Doctors	Mother
Cold	Warmth	Cloth

As we grow, and accumulate experience, our information environment grows:

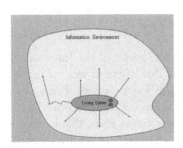

Family
Home
Places
Siblings
Neighborhoods
Friends
Relatives
Sounds

Elementary School expands our horizons still further and brings more information with it.

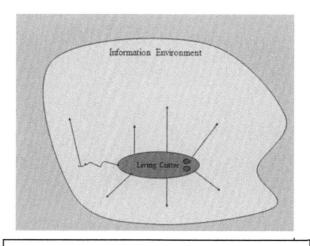

School

Classmates

Information Learned

Rules

Outside Experiences

Individualization

Individuals at a Distance

News

Internet

Project/Learning Work

Middle and high school give us our first adult experience and reach, including more autonomy.

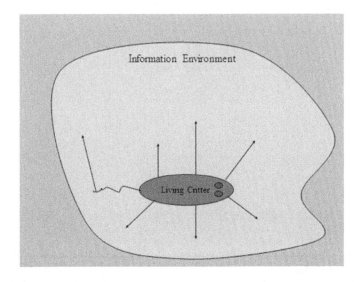

Purpose
Clubs
Disciplines of Learning
Social Activity
Travel
Expanded Internet Use
World Knowledge (News)
Anxiety and Peer Pressure

Adolescent Struggle
Work
Arts
Enjoy Learning
Planning
Responsibility
Self Reflection
Experience

Adulthood brings with it the full range of being human, for good or for ill, and the expansion of the individual Information Environment continues throughout life. (Ours is constantly expanding, with no end in sight.)

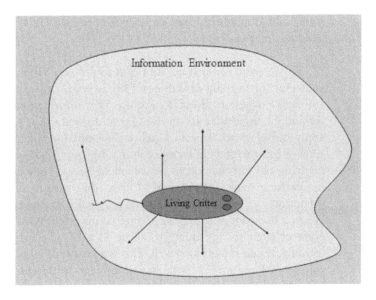

Interestingly, this set of graphics suggests a real opportunity for us to "time travel" by talking with older individuals and tapping into their experiences and the lessons that they have learned. We can also "time travel" and perspective shift by talking with younger people.

Growth by replacing old ideas with new ones proceeds best when a path of incremental addition is followed – though sometimes discontinuous breaks are called for (Art, Science, Mathematics, Technology and so on). Incremental addition is when new information gets added to an old idea and the result is an expanded view of what was previously known. A discontinuous break occurs when the new ideas are so dissimilar to the old ones that a completely new idea is formed, perhaps containing some parts of the old idea, but being fundamentally new. New ideas derived from experience with things outside the learner – or studies or readings in Art, Science, and Mathematics. Interactions with outside experiences can be discontinuous or, if they are expansions of already-ongoing development, continuous. This may sound like double-talk, but we learn by growing and that's what this means.

As we grow and mature, we begin to develop habits and strategies for learning new things. "In the wild," our natural curiosity pushes us ahead to acquire new information. In school, the imperative to survive and to do well drives us to apply ourselves to "learning" school information, often by storing information in memory and retrieving it, often by applying old information to new challenges, and sometimes by crafting new information. Often this means doing "schoolwork," which may or may not make sense to us. When it does not, true organic learning is impeded. When we connect what we are doing to some idea of what we are learning, things move along well. This is all very complex, but can be analyzed into its separate components, differentiated by purpose.

Fortunately, there is a set of strategies that can enhance and promote effective learning. Each of them has been time-tested and is used to one degree or another by effective learners. Academically struggling learners in college, for instance, show high levels of anxiety. They also show weakness in concentration, motivation, identifying main ideas and time management (Proctor et al., 2006). Learners getting targeted instruction in study skills tend to show improved grades, test scores and SATs (Robyak, 1978). As you can see, these things have been known for a long time.

Moreover, learners of intermediate ability profit the most from this instruction (Entwistle, 1960). These effects are notable in notetaking, summarization, and re-reading strategies (Dyer et al., 1979). It is amazing that we have known these things for so long and that so very few learners have had directed instruction in learning strategies. More recent studies support the earlier research conclusions. Note-taking ability is among the many factors at play in learning (Siegel, 2022).

The purpose of this chapter is to explain these skills and strategies for the reader and to show how each may be used. Each of them may be modified in use and may be extended to serve learners throughout life.

What Learning Strategies/Study Skills are For

The strategies below are to be used when interacting with the Information Environment to gain information for future or immediate use. They tend to be the traditional approaches used by successful learners and scholars. They can be used either in or out of "class." And electronics such as computers, tablets and iPads may be incorporated into them, using the principles explained below.

Your Interaction with the Information Environment

Each of the skills outlined below interacts with the others and strengthens connections of information conducive to long-term learning. You control their use, and this determines their effectiveness in serving your learning purposes and goals. Just as your Information Environment is the result of your personal ongoing experience, the results of applying each skill provide slightly different results in different situations.

LSMNTI – the Big Six. This is an acronym for the six areas whose mastery contributes to successful and purposeful learning are:

Listening
Scheduling (Time Management)
Memory
Note-Taking
Textbooks (and other information sources)
Information Use

These are skills that most people will agree are important. They have been a part of scholarship since time immemorial. They are still of primary importance in our current era of technologically-mediated information and for the foreseeable future. Successful learners master them (Kartika, 2007). All told, however, the number of people who master all of them is very low compared to what it might be. That's why most school grade distributions look a good bit like the normal curve. An individual's skill at learning, retaining, retrieving and using information has a powerful effect on success (Crede & Kuncel, 2008). While it may be thought that these are taught in school, this is not necessarily so. While the number of my learners who need their listening skills to acquire information is very high, the number with prior instruction in listening skills in schools is fairly low. The same can be said of the other skill areas. Learning and practicing a few specific skills can improve your academic experience, your "learning in the wild," and your success in life.

Listening

Listening well is key in learning and living well, yet it is not practiced by all and contributes to much miscommunication and misinformation. Since it has such a direct effect on our success, it is important to be able to listen well.

And yet listening in school and in life is assumed to be a well-developed skill, even though little directed attention and instruction are invested in it. Often I ask my classes, "How many of you have had identifiable instruction in listening along the way?" Usually two or at most three out of 28 respond that they have. When I ask what this looked like, none of them can remember. When I suggest to my classes that they don't listen well, many individuals act offended.

And the proof is in the pudding. Throughout the semester, I often have to repeat answers to the simplest questions, such as "What's going to be on the exam?" (The exam is posted on the second day of class and explained to all learners.) Another favorite is "When is the final exam due to be submitted?" (That's on the slide with the final, posted online and on the presentation slide shown on day 2 of class and carefully pointed out to learners.)

These questions are predictable each semester. It's just a matter of when someone will ask them. Sad but true. And poor listening or attention to course requirements is a great influence of final grades.

In their research on listening, Spataro and Bloch (2018) note that, "listening is a critical part of communication …. Active listening surpasses passive listening or simple hearing to establish a deeper connection between speaker and listener, as the listener gives the speaker full attention via inquiry, reflection, respect, and empathy" (p. 168).

Dr. Ralph Nichols, founder of the International Listening Association, offers some advice. Nichols (1957) says at the end of a 10-minute lecture most college freshmen will have retained only half of it. Then, 48 hours later they will have forgotten half of what they remembered. He suggests ten ways to listen to boring lectures:

1. Choose to find the subject useful
2. Concentrate on the words and message, not the speaker

3. Hold your fire before responding and stay tuned into the speaker, not yourself
4. Identify the "big ideas"
5. Adjust your note taking to the speaker's pattern
6. Work hard to stay attentive
7. Aggressively tackle difficult material

8. Don't let emotionally charged "buzzwords" tune you out
9. Get to know the speaker personally
10. Use the differential between speed of speech and speed of thinking

These 10 items of advice are still relevant today, but we'll add a few more.

11. Don't let technology distract you
12. Don't let anything else distract you
13. Summarize what you've just heard in order to fix it in memory
14. Decide on what use you will make of what you've heard
15. Establish methods of storing information

These items are relevant to today's learners, as the pace of things has sped up and technology in all of its forms has become overwhelmingly present in our lives. The 15 items above present good advice for those wishing to be active learners.

> "Never sit in the back of the class. Period."
> -Third-Year Student

So, how do you work to improve your listening?

First, get a feel for how good your current listening is. Do you gain the information you want and need from talking with people? Do you learn well from lectures and presentations in class? Are you happy with what you get from listening to family and friends? If the answers to these are "OK" to "not very," you may want to take steps to improve your abilities to focus, listen and recall.

Second, choose a listening situation you encounter on a regular basis. At the end of each session, rate yourself on how well you listened with respect to the 15 items above. Go ahead, make yourself a scorecard and use it for five sessions, completing it after each session.

At the end of each session, rate yourself on each challenge dimension. Use any scoring system you like but keep it consistent. For instance, score yourself with a zero, a minus or a plus. Or give yourself a grade A through F. At the end of 5 days, calculate your average scores. Then, selecting one to work on, enter "work on" in the comments column on the scorecard.

Work on that challenge for another five days, as indicated after the table. At the end of that time, you should see an improvement, if you have been applying yourself. If not, you have a decision to make. Continue, seek help, or select another challenge. We recommend that you start with an easy one first.

See suggestions after the chart for how to work to improve certain challenges.

LEARN LIKE A DRAGON

	Listening Challenge	1	2	3	4	5	AVG
1	Finding Subject Interesting/Useful						
2	Distracted by Speaker						
3	Argumentative/Self Absorbed						
4	Finding Big Ideas						
5	Noting According to Speaker's Pattern						
6	Not Working at Listening						
7	Not Tackling Difficult Ideas						
8	Tuned Out by Buzz Words						
9	Keeping Speaker One-Dimensional						
10	Not Using the Differential for Thinking/Listening						
11	Technological Distractions						
12	Other Distractions						
13	Need to Summarize						
14	Establish Usefulness of Information						
15	Find Ways to Store Information						

Another way of going about listening improvement is focusing on it each day at a standard time. In my classes, I showed the learners the challenges. Then I told them we'd be returning to them for each class to evaluate progress. First, I had them be aware of when they were aware of challenges. That took 7 or so classes. Then I had learners tell us about their learning episode and what they did to meet their listening challenge. We did this for the next 36 class sessions, taking 5 minutes or so at the beginning of class to have 3 volunteers share their experiences with us. I constantly told them to look for listening challenges at the end of each class, so that they could share at the beginning of the next. After 8 or so classes, they got the message that this was not going away.

Result? At semester's end a sizable percentage mentioned increased listening ability as one of the key benefits of the course. I tend to believe them. Do you?

It takes effort to work on listening improvement until it's habitual – and it's truly a lifetime task. But it's a lifetime task worth undertaking.

Scheduling (Time Management – Sound Familiar?)

Scheduling and time management were covered in glorious detail in the previous chapter. They are critical in giving you control of your time and productivity and their importance cannot be overrated. Keep the following in mind.

- Your actions and accomplishments make you who you are
- Scheduling and managing your time allow the previous bullet point to be under your control
- Having and managing priorities and actions allows you to retrench and replan when encountering obstacles

- Looking ahead helps you identify upcoming obstacles and to preplan alternative actions
- Staying focused on your priorities through time keeps you on course
- Careful planning allows you to reserve time for yourself, for health, recreation, travel and play
- You need to refocus your vision and intentions every day
- You should reconsider your plans every week
- You should have a major "think session" at least once a month
- You should keep plans and schedules in a manner that allows for easy alteration
- You should keep a backup copy of your plan/calendar – and keep it current (most printers today are also copiers, and you can scan or photograph a copy for storage)
- It is easier to stick to your plan when you have one
- Success at planning goes hand in hand with success in executing it – and in meeting your goals
- The unexamined life is not worth living. The unplanned life is also not worth living
- Life as it comes at us is not particularly unchaotic; a plan can help us make sense of things
- Nothing promotes good sleep as well as a good plan
- Planning defeats procrastination – start today and procrastinate tomorrow
- Start your plan now and review it as soon as you can, in whatever stage it is in
- As President Eisenhower once said, "Plans are nothing; planning is everything" – planning is dynamic and ongoing
- So get busy.

Memory

Memory is your ability to recall and to use your past experience. It is extremely complex, both neurologically and procedurally. Your recall is composed of an edited representation of past experience – not an exact copy. Moreover, experience can be encoded as it occurs in order to facilitate enhanced recall later on. There are many means for doing so.

Much of what we call memory requires that we be specific about the circumstances of recoding and retrieval and the uses to which we intend to put what we recall. When we have an experience, our perceptual systems feed sensory data to our cognitive and visual faculties, which encode them to memory traces, which consist of neural cell subassemblies which have coordinated probabilities of excitation.

When a memory needs to be recalled, recall signals are sent to the subassemblies, which return a translation of the experience to our cognitive or visual faculties, which results in meaning being made. Notice that the sensory experience goes through a great many transformations, which are currently poorly understood.

Nonetheless, we gain conscious awareness of the experience in a meaningful way, which means that the information recalled fits as truth into our awareness and understanding of reality. This occurs very rapidly. Of course, if "memories" are older or more deeply encoded, it can take more time and some effort to retrieve them. That's why, in general, our memory recall slows down as we age, but all of our memories are intact, ready for retrieval. Except, as we age, we "clean house" and toss memories that we deem to be unnecessary. Consistent use of our storage and retrieval faculties can reduce this effect and, in many cases, eliminate it entirely.

In short, our memory works like a filing cabinet. Our perceptions take in information from the outside and "file" it in the form of meaningful ideas. It indexes it and recodes it into a set of cell subassemblies. When we recall something, the meaning is retrieved from the file – somewhat edited, but intact.

The thing to remember is that you can improve your memory through the use of various strategies (Higbee, 2001). The key to improving your recall is that of following a process that increases the number of memory traces at the time of experience, at the time of "study" (affixing hooks to the memory to facilitate recall), practice, and spaced maintenance activity. The process overview is as follows:

Attention
Predisposition
Encoding Work ("Learning" – recognizing and storing)
Rehearsal
Self-Testing
Maintenance

Following this process cuts across all traditional learning and study methods and includes the effective elements of many of them.

Attention

Enter each learning experience with a focused, open and alert mind. Live your life this way if you can. You apprehend that to which you attend. Maintain an open mind and you will absorb as much as possible – you can move toward storing what you deem important and discard the rest. (You experience many things not worth the effort of storing.)

Before entering upon a learning for recall experience, take a cleansing breath to clear and quiet your mind (Kabat-

Zinn, 2005). Make yourself as alert as possible. This is a habit worth cultivating (Nhat Hanh, 2005). Open the doors of your mind and perhaps call to mind the categories in which you think you might be dealing. Sometimes you'll be right, sometimes not. But when you are not, you'll hear the bell of cognitive dissonance in your head and can switch gears to better categories, or just leave the baffles wide open and build a category name from the information you perceive.

Notice when your attention flags, if it does, and do a redirect or move to a different activity; you may be done with this experience. This advice runs throughout your experience.

Predisposition

"Sell" the learning to yourself. Think something like "I'm going to learn _____, OK?" and answer with "yes." Even if you don't feel like it, set this intention. If you cannot, do something else until you really need to return to your effort. There's no crime in setting something aside, because you can return later, but remember: feigning interest often turns into the real thing and is good enough for what you are doing. Declaring something to be interesting and then acting as though this is true often becomes a self-fulfilling prophecy. There is often a reason for buckling down in this way – say progress toward mastering a field you need to master.

Once, we asked three sections of our classes what their least interesting course happened to be. 80% of them mentioned a key course in their major which they were taking. We suggested to them that they were in the wrong major – or that they should adjust their predisposition to master whatever was at hand. This didn't go over well, but this didn't make it an untrue observation. We suspect that many of them shifted gears. More than 30 percent of college students switch majors at least once (National Center for Education Statistics, 2017), and some switch more times than that!

Encoding Work (and Memory Strategies)

This is where you work to increase the number of memory traces associated with what you are learning. There are many ways to do this. Our advice is to use as many as possible, increasing the number as the information becomes more slippery or more important. There are things that you must use brute force to encode for recall, and these tend to be things which carry no meaning or make no sense to you. Since your memory is not a logical thing, you may use various encoding methods to trap this information. Make the information into a rhyme, a rap, a drawing, an image, a sketch or perhaps a loud sound.

Repeating something to yourself several times often helps, since you must be able to form the words carrying the information. This means speak it out loud. There are software programs that will speak aloud the text you highlight. You should do this so that you have an accurate auditory representation of it – and this includes mathematical and scientific formulas and notation. So, say or read the information to yourself several times. It won't hurt; it may not do the trick, but it is necessary for you to master the information. This, by the way, is essential if you are working on a presentation; a good way to destroy the value of your work is to mispronounce important words (any words that make the audience do a double take). Sometimes trusting this method for later recall betrays you. "In one ear and out the other" often describes the results, but it's a start.

Visualizing information as you take it in helps with adding memory traces to the information you want to capture and store. Pictures are memorable because of this. Think about the art you know – Mona Lisa and others. You have a pretty good grasp on them because visual information is rich and lends itself to memory traces and hooks.

Drawing a picture of the information is a great idea. Put it in your notes. Then label it. "Ear," in this case. Adds information to the information you experience and makes it more memorable. By the way, you don't have to be an artist, great or otherwise, to do this. I get by with diagrams and stick figures, some of them laughable, but I don't care – they work to enhance memorability. I regularly get laughed at for the pictures and diagrams I draw on the whiteboard in class, but I don't care. The laughter boosts memorability. You can even make visual puns, which makes things more powerful. Below see a visual representation for the concept of listening.

Our students do an activity called "Keepers" at the beginning and end of class. I visualize this activity thus:

Add the images together and you get "keepers" = "key" + "purrs." Get it? Anyway, it's fun if you can do it. Most people can once they catch on. Some people don't. Which are you?

You can add one picture to another in your mind's eye – they will "stick together" and comprise a recallable sequence, even after only a few rehearsals (three is a good start, although the more the merrier). This is called *"visual chaining,"* and it has been a mainstay of memorizers for ages (see Higbee, 2001 for specific strategies). If you are going to the store for groceries, visualize your grocery list: milk, butter, eggs, bread, cauliflower, soda, popcorn, cheese, enchilada sauce, and so on. See a picture of a carton of milk. See a stick of butter, and then slide it over so that it touches the milk carton (click!) and continue the process. Rehearse it 3 times and head for the store. When you get there, visualize the milk and then look at what is stuck to it, and so on. This works reasonably well. Of course, a list captured to your phone often works better, but this method works if you don't have your phone with you.

You can also store incoming information on a mental set of "hooks," which have their own internal integrity and serve as ordered spaces into which to put ideas. This is much the same way that computers work to store information in memory and memory chips. Each chunk of information gets its own "pigeonhole" and can always be recalled when that pigeonhole is accessed.

A simple set of memory hooks can be conceptualized as follows – a coat rack with numbered hooks.

In kindergarten, for instance, Kid #1's coat goes on hook 1, Kid #2's coat goes on hook 2, and so on. When you want the coat back, you get it from the appropriate hook. All you need to remember is which hook you need to access. This works for one to a zillion coats – or ideas.

There is no inherent meaning to the hook numbers, so we can add to their memorability by assigning images to each one.

In the diagram above, each "peg" has been assigned an associated image (which can be random, but which here "rhymes," further enhancing recallability).

Sun
Shoe
Tree
Door
Hive
Stick
Heaven
Plate
Vine
Hen

Each rhymes with its number, from one to ten. Above ten, you begin chaining images, so 37 is an image that blends tree with heaven. It runs forever.

To use it, you "attach" or chain your first idea to the first image. Then you "attach" your second idea to the second image, and so on. The method adds the power of number sequence memory to rhyming (up through 10) memory, to imagery and its associated recall power. It is very simple to use with a little practice. I use it for speeches and presentations and the sequence of activities in class. I simply turn each activity into a picture and run through it in my head a couple of times, and I'm ready to go.

Suppose I wanted to memorize the 10 Commandments of Good Listening (or you did, since I memorized them in 1980 and still recall them).

First I list them on paper or in my mind's eye, then I attach them to the pegs, then I rehearse. Before I present, I rehearse again.

The 10 Commandments of Good Listening according to Ralph Nichols are:

1. Choose to find the subject useful
2. Concentrate on the words and message, not the speaker
3. Hold your fire before responding. And say tuned into the speaker, not yourself
4. Identify the "big ideas"
5. Adjust your note taking to the speaker's pattern
6. Work hard to stay attentive
7. Aggressively tackle difficult material
8. Don't let emotionally charged "buzzwords" tune you out
9. Get to know the speaker personally
10. Use the differential between speed of speech and speed of thinking

LEARN LIKE A DRAGON

> "I learned a lot about how to learn in this class. I plan to take research, tips, and ethical frameworks and apply it as a teacher in my classroom next year—especially the 'Ten Commandments of Good Listening.' In the words of Mr. Dewey, 'education is life itself.'" -Fourth-Year Student

First, I make images for each concept:

1. Cartoon character pointing at a menu
2. Character looking at a page of text with a microscope
3. Candle with flame
4. Shopping Cart w/ "Big Ideas" sign
5. Page of DaVinci Notes
6. Character lifting barbell
7. Character in football uniform tackling someone
8. Buzz saw blade with "x" through it
9. Character shaking hands with speaker at podium
10. Two speedometers at different speeds

The images can be very simple. Very. They merely represent ideas.

1. Cartoon character pointing at a menu

2. Looking at a page of text with a microscope

3. Candle with flame

4. Shopping Cart w/ "Big Ideas" sign

5. Page of DaVinci Notes

6. Character lifting barbell

7. Character in football uniform tackling someone

8. Buzz saw blade with "x" through it

9. Character shaking hands with speaker at podium

10. Two speedometers at different speeds

Now, I visualize each image peg (bun, shoe, tree, and so on) with each meaning image attached.

Sun with menu pointer
Show with microscope + book
Tree with candles and so on.

We form the clearest image we can, "gaze" at it for a couple of seconds, then move on.

Then we review all ten compound images. Recalling the number gives me the peg image, recalling that pulls the meaning image into mind, and then we can talk about the commandment of good listening.

Sounds complicated? It may require a few steps, but it's simple and fluid in operation. Try it and you'll see.

Last but not least, there's the method of locations, which became the memory palace technique in the European Middle Ages (and which was first described in Cicero's book on Rhetoric, written in 47 BCE).

First a story. A Greek philosopher named Simonides is cited as the originator of this by Cicero. Simonides was delivering a poem at a banquet when he was called outside. As he was talking with the men who had summoned him, there was an earthquake which collapsed the building he had just left. By visualizing the banquet and its attendees, he was able to recall their names. Hence, the method of location is first cited.

If you look carefully at a place, you'll be able to recreate it in your mind (and even to sketch it). A classroom, a lecture hall, your bedroom or kitchen, a room in a library. Then you identify various components in the room. You turn your ideas into images and post (attach) each image to one element of the room. This is the method used by Cicero during Roman times. Later on, it was realized that one room could indeed be just one of many in a palace or a home or a building, and the concept of Memory Palace was born. You could store enormous amounts of information by storing images in various places.

As writing and notes became more commonplace, this fell out of use, since there were other ways of storing and retrieving information (books and notes, for instance) and making long speeches from memory was no longer a task that cemented one's civic power in the minds of listeners. Politicians, of course, can make use of this, but most of them use teleprompters or notes these days, and they tend not to be that long-winded anymore. Well, most of them. Nor so good at speaking that we watch them for entertainment.

You can, of course, use the method of location to store information in preparation for an exam, oral or written, but it should be used for important occasions.

Remembering things is important. You should always work to store and recall facts, because that is how useful dialogue and discourse are conducted. Facts are important, and you should be able to recall them and their sources in everyday and in academic life.

Rehearsal

If you have worked to store information for later use, you should rehearse recalling it from time to time. Once a week, perhaps, or once a month, particularly if it is information you will use. Of course, if you have things written down, you can simply refer to that, but for thinking on your feet, it is often useful to have the material "on the tip of your tongue." Rehearsals should be entered onto your ongoing calendar and scheduled for regular intervals.

Self-Testing

To check the effectiveness of your work with recall, you should test yourself to see if you can do it. This is a useful precursor to review and study. If you work to remember something, you should be sure that you can. This is great before tests, both academic and life tests. If you don't do it, you don't use your memory faculty, and forgetting (inability to recall) accelerates.

Maintenance

From time to time, as noted above, you should review and practice recall. Spaced maintenance over time promotes strong retention abilities. In addition, get a good night's rest because sleep helps your brain consolidate new learning (Tonomi & Cirelli, 2014).

Conclusion

With the Dragon Mindset, you can navigate the Information Environment using key listening skills and memory tips. These are powerful concepts that demonstrate the importance of "input and storage" skills and how to improve them. These are the foundations of all future learning. Work on them early in your learning career, or start now. As the Dragon says, "Procrastinate Tomorrow!"

References

Credé, M., & Kuncel, N. R. (2008). Study habits, skills, and attitudes: The third pillar supporting collegiate academic performance. *Perspectives on Psychological Science, 3*(6), 425–453. https://doi.org/10.1111/j.1745-6924.2008.00089

Dyer, J. W., Riley, J. D., & Yekovich, F. R. (1979). An analysis of three study skills: Notetaking, summarizing, and rereading. *Journal of Educational Research, 73*(1), 3-7.

Entwistle, N. (1960). Evaluation of study skills courses. *Journal of Educational Research, 53,* 243-251.

Higbee, K. L. (2001). *Your memory: How it works and how to improve it.* Da Capo Lifelong Books.

Kabat-Zinn, J. (2005). *Wherever you go, there you are.* Hachette Books.

Kartika, A. (2007). Study skills training: Is it an answer to the lack of college students' study skills? *The International Journal of Learning, 14*(9), 35-43.

National Center for Education Statistics. (2017). *Percentage of 2011–12 first time postsecondary students who had ever declared a major in an associate's or bachelor's degree program within 3 years of enrollment.* Institute of Education Sciences, U.S. Department of Education. https://nces.ed.gov/pubs2018/2018434.pdf

Nhat Hanh, T. (2005). *Being peace.* Parallax Press.

Proctor, B., Prevatt, F., Adams, K., Hurst, A., & Petscher, Y. (2006). Study skills profiles of normal-achieving and academically-struggling college students. *Journal of College Student Development, 47*(1). http://dx.org/10.1353/csd.2006.0011

Robyak, J. (1978). Study skills versus non-study skills students: A discriminant analysis. *The Journal of Education Research, 71,* 161–166.

Siegel, J. (2022). Factors affecting notetaking performance. *International Journal of Listening*, 1-13. https://doi.org/10.1080/10904018.2022.2059484

Spataro, S. E., & Bloch, J. (2018). "Can you repeat that?": Teaching active listening in management education. *Journal of Management Education, 42*(2), 168–198. https://doi.org/10.1177/1052562917748696

Tononi, G., & Cirelli, C. (2014). Sleep and the price of plasticity: From synaptic and cellular homeostasis to memory consolidation and integration. *Neuron, 81*(1), 12-34. doi: 10.1016/j.neuron.2013.12.025.

CHAPTER 3
SOARING WITH THE ENHANCED DAVINCI NOTETAKING SYSTEM©

Jack Cole

"The noblest pleasure is the joy of understanding."
— Leonardo da Vinci

I first encountered notetaking in 1957, when I entered third grade. The directions were to write what you are told in your notebook. Words, math facts and exercises, what's on the board, and that was about it. It was direction-based. When the direction stopped, so did I. It wasn't even good handwriting practice. This continued for years.

In eighth grade, I was told to take notes from lectures and visuals in preparation for a test. That's all we were told, and I never got very good at it. When the teacher said, "Take notes, y'all," that didn't include the details of how to do it. So I didn't improve.

High school was different. We were expected to take notes in History, Science and English, and they were collected, inspected, and graded. In general, more was better. However, I had no way to write, except laboriously, and no guidance as to what to write, except for what I thought was important or what might be on a test. And copying lists that would be tested. Since I had a facile mind, I usually guessed correctly, but they were guesses.

No one told me to look at a textbook for hints as to what might be important, or to divine the structure of the information (an alien concept until half-past graduate school, years later). So, notes in high school were sporadic, no matter how "good" the instruction we received.

College was a challenge for me. I tried underlining books, but taking notes from lectures, labs or experiences escaped me. I bought many notebooks (one for each subject, of course), but left all but the first 10 pages or so empty at the end of a semester. Writing was hard, and listening was harder. At new student orientation, we were told to take notes, but that was all. This was even before the days when learners were prompted to keep a journal.

This was the same in my Master's program. My notes from that era were minimal and of minimal use. Information did seem to stick better, and underlining texts helped more, since I had a better grasp of the structure of things. Then, I was struck by lightning during the second half of my doctoral program, when I received a graduate assistantship at the Reading and Study Skills Lab at the University of Maryland, College Park. The counselors there strongly emphasized taking good notes, and they used a 3-column system developed by Walter Pauk of Cornell University.

> "One aspect of the course that I want to comment on is the note taking style that was implemented this semester. I found that the notes I took in this class were some of the best notes out of my entire college experience. I specifically liked the GAOSS and "keepers" aspects of the notes. Writing these made it super helpful to look back onto class sessions and remember what we talked about in discussion and presentations. I felt as though grasping the material was made so much easier with these effective note taking strategies and that I remembered so much more than if I had not taken notes in this way. These are skills that I will use in the future for my master's program and career." -Second Year Student

Pauk's system required the learner to divide the page into 3 columns – 15%, 70% and 15%, more or less. The center column was used to record "running notes" (write down anything worth remembering). The left-hand column was used for Key Words (titles for the running notes, important terms, directions or assignment markers) and the right-hand column was to be used for summarizing the session, so the learner only wrote one per class, at the end.

The theory was that the running notes kept the learner focused and captured information for later, the key word column fostered higher-level real-time processing of the running notes, and the summary provided a high-level overview of the session to facilitate later recall of the whole experience. Pauk suggested that, done well, 75-80% of the answers on true/false, matching, fill-in, short answer and multiple-choice answers would appear in the Key Word column and that 75% of the essay questions on exams could be predicted by simply rewriting the Summaries as essay questions.

In practice, this worked fairly well. Exam preparation consisted of reading the Summary for a day's class and then trying to recall the Key Words for the day. Key Words escaping recall were to be learned for recall later. Learners were to try to remember the running notes and details pertinent to each Key Word, again, studying material that had escaped their recall. And, of course, learners were counseled to turn each Summary into three essay questions and to craft a brief outline for each, to be filled from the rest of the notes (and readings) and to be crafted as an essay at the time of the test. Again, research is scarce on how this worked, but anecdotal evidence supports the notion that this system was effective. Research has increased in specificity and quality since then, and generally shows good results.

This was called the Cornell Notes System and was adopted widely in my home state of Maryland. And it foundered and failed widely in the years since the 1980s when it was imposed on schools without adequate preparation.

Why? It was not understood by some educators, even to the degree outlined in the few brief paragraphs above. It was, therefore, imposed on teachers, who sabotaged what they could not support. When taught, it was poorly taught and not followed up with critique, comments or useful suggestions. Lecture remains the least effective – and most used – method of "teaching." Things that are taught are not caught, due to listening skills not being effectively dealt with in school. And because it was boring the way it turned out. Too much work for too little return, too. But I used it as soon as I saw and learned it, it worked for me, although I made a few modifications to the system and renamed it to make it a new way of working. The current version I use – and require of my classes for those learners who want to excel – is called the Enhanced DaVinci Notetaking System©.

THE ENHANCED DAVINCI NOTETAKING SYSTEM©

A sample page of the current system looks more or less like this.

Taking Notes

Key Words Go Here:	1. Stream of Consciousness	Summarize at end of session: CAOSS
Remember Highlight Time Sequence	Ideas Concepts Thoughts Figures/Drawings/Doodles Quotations 1-2-3's a-b-c's Just keep writing Capture all thoughts Stay awake < key word as you go	

Column A   Column B   Column C

The page itself consists of 3 columns. Learners draw them on each page. This sets their intention to use parts of the page for different purposes.

- Column A is for Key Words
- Column B is for Running Notes
- Column C is for Summary, but it runs sideways, with the page rotated 90 degrees, from left to right.

See the example below.

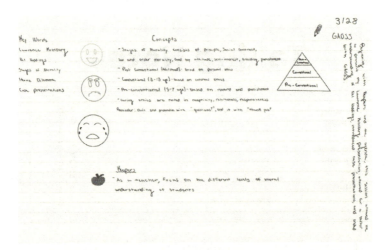

I made a few modifications in the Cornell Notes to produce the Enhance DaVinci Notetaking System©, as follows:

Column A is for Key Words. In this column, make Titles for the material in your running notes. Use words or icons or pictures, as above in the Memory section. These give more structure to your running notes and help ideas stick for later use. Develop a system for marking ideas: stars (asterisks), exclamation points, check marks, light bulbs, targets, sketches of calendars, and abbreviations (DD = due date, DNF = do not forget, PN = phone number, ID = important date, and so on). Your Key Words mirror the running notes and help form a structure for your thinking. Do Key Words while taking Running Notes and during lulls in the action. You'll be glad you did.

Column B is the Running Notes section of the page. In this section, you keep writing during the session, from beginning to end. Write down information you think will be important. It is encouraged to guess. What's important to you? What's important to the speaker? What do you think might be on a test or quiz? What strikes you as needing to be remembered later? Why not write down random thoughts? That way, they don't disappear.

Use single words, phrases, and abbreviations. Do not write complete sentences, unless you are capturing a complete quotation – and then, you are better to abbreviate things and return later to fill this out. Usually, quotations are illusive. If they appear on a screen or a whiteboard or on a slide, take a picture of them with your camera and insert them in your notes at your leisure.

Use sequence markers such as 1, 2, 3 or A., B., C. or I, II, III. Do this particularly when the speaker indicates to you that a series of things is to come.

Draw pictures of ideas in your Running Notes. You can doodle, copy pictures from elsewhere, or sketch things or diagrams. Three per page is a good target. Information sticks to pics, as we say. Use color if you like. Using color coding is a good idea in general. Invent your own system. They make taking notes more enjoyable and fun.

Write down any ideas you have – whether they pertain to the subject at hand or not. You want to capture ideas for later, whether they are pertinent or just good ideas you have. You don't want to lose them. These may include do-lists for later, recipes or poems, bright ideas or plans for research papers or presentations. Add phone numbers, notes to classmates, lightning bolts, targets, or anything you like. Your notes are your notes; what's in them is your business and no one else's.

Work to make your notes pretty by decorating your pages. If anyone questions you, tell them that "illuminated manuscripts" are more memorable and that your notes are a memory aid that works by elaboration. Decorate away, since artwork belongs in your notes. Art has been a primary memory tool since humans developed language (Fernandes et al., 2018). Artists also play a key role in sketching out, or dreaming up, our future.

Write, write, write and sketch, sketch, sketch. It becomes easier with time. I often put things in my notes that seem to have nothing to do with the topics at hand. That's where my creativity comes in, and I begin to make new connections between ideas.

Column C is for your Summary of the session. Most of us were never taught to write a proper summary, and most of us do not like writing summaries, myself included. Until, one day, in my graduate study, lightning struck! I bumped into an article by Silver Stanfill, then a professor at Anchorage Community College. The article was entitled, "The Great American One Sentence Summary (GAOSS)." She stated that it's possible to summarize any experience with one sentence. It's a patterned sentence.

Always goes the same way. Don't fool with it. Like this:

"Beginning with _____, _____ did _____, did _____, did _____, and ended with _____."

Simple, eh? It can apply to anything. For example, "Beginning with a botched pitch in the first inning, the Orioles batted horribly, fielded like Little Leaguers, complained bitterly and ended with a loss of 79-8."

We tend to remember things in three's (Cowan, 2001). It just works. So, with Column C, turn your page sideways to the left and write the summary. One per session. Works like a charm.

THE ENHANCED DAVINCI NOTETAKING SYSTEM©

When you want to study for an exam or quiz:

1. Read the GAOSS. Turn the clauses into essay questions and try to answer them. Make a brief outline for each. Then, try to recall the day's Key Words.
2. Look at the Key Words. Any that you have recalled, you're basically done studying. You have that information as answers to true/false, multiple choice, fill-in, and short-answer questions. Study and commit

to memory those you have forgotten.
3. From the Key Words, try to recall your associated Running Notes. For those that you recall, you're done. For those that you do not, study and retain.
4. Repeat 1-3, ideally right before the quiz or exam.

Note that with this method of review and study, you only spend significant time on material you don't already know or remember. Try this: walk the hall at exam time and look at the people you see studying. They tend to review the stuff they already know instead of testing themselves on material that they have forgotten, which usually isn't in their notes. How smart is that? How many extra points does that get them?

By the way, studying with a partner or two is a great idea. Quiz each other and fill in gaps in your notes as you go. It's a great system, but it may take a little work to get it to work for you.

1. Start with running notes for a couple of classes and fill in Key Words and GAOSS at the end
2. Take running notes
3. Fill in Key Words as you go
4. Do GAOSS at the end
5. Do all four steps. Repeat for 7-8 classes and it'll become second nature.
6. Expand this method to your other classes

> "I really enjoyed this course and learned a lot this semester. My biggest takeaway is the Da Vinci Note Taking System. I have been using this method for almost all my classes. It is extremely helpful and keeps all my notes organized. I will definitely continue to use this note-taking method when I need it for the rest of my life. I have seen more improvements in my grades after using this in my other classes." -Second-Year Student

Work with a friend or group to master this. Teachers: notice that it takes ongoing attention before it becomes natural and habitual. The time you spend with this over a couple of months will pay off handsomely. Students will learn more and stay tuned in better. Everyone wins.

Feel free to modify the format to fit yourself once you have mastered the basics. When is this? A little while after you figure you have. As they say, "Don't practice until you get it right; practice until you can't do it wrong." Good advice. The Dragons agree with this.

Information and Its Uses

We already know that we get through college and life by accumulating and using information. In college, much of the usage involves recalling it and using it on academic tasks: quizzes, exams, dialogue, papers and written assignments. That's a very small slice of potential information use.

Information has value. You can even calculate it. Take your car for a repair, and it may cost you $750. Go to the hospital for brain surgery and you (or your health insurance) may pay $75,000. Or call a plumber on the weekend and pay $300. You are paying for information in use. All of these people know things you do not. You're paying for their knowledge.

In college, you pay tuition. So our course may cost you 1/6 of your $7000 tuition for the semester or, since we have 43 sessions, or about $27.12 per 50-minute session. If you come away with 3 ideas you didn't have before, each one is worth $9.04. See how this works? Information has value. But, when you skip a class, you're wasting a good bit of money. Show your parents this calculation, and they won't be amused. In college, you can use this information for a restricted number of purposes. The more you retain, the higher your grade if you use it well.

It's the same in life and on the job. Except that the uses are different (and each one uses a format like GAOSS, only different), so when you organize the information into the format, you have a professional information product with real value.

The Ways People Write Should Affect the Ways You Read

I once asked several classes of public relations and marketing specialists in the Master of Science in Marketing Course I taught at Johns Hopkins University what sort of writing they did on the job, and the list was extensive. It included:

Press releases
Media alerts
Talking points for events
Newsletters
Magazine articles
Advertising copy
Status reports
Op-ed pieces
Pitches for the media
Marketing plans
Timelines
Meeting agendas
Public service announcements
Flyers
Posters
Banners
Fundraising letters

Each of these information products has real value, and they rest on the knowledge base of the professional crafting it! Use headings and topic markers to enhance your retention, note-taking and recall.

So, what use is information? Vast and varied – and the list above only refers to professionals in the fields of marketing, project management and marketing management! Multiply it by several professional fields, and it becomes vast.

Look at it through the lens of the profession you are to enter, and it's impressive. Even look at what you deal with as a citizen or family member and it's fairly long (news articles, taxes, correspondence, email, loan documents, auto purchase contracts, bids from contractors, and on and on). As you collect information, remind yourself what it will be used to do. That helps you to understand and select.

Remember that each of these information products has a format. Identify the elements of the format needed in each task you do, and the task will flow more easily. Each task may be analyzed into its components. Professionals use them extensively, and so should you.

Conclusion

The Enhanced DaVinci Notetaking System© is a powerful way to master your Information Environment and learn like a Dragon. The Dragons say that mastery of even one part of it and using the skills outlined will enhance your capacities as a learner, a student, and a worker. Work through and implement one part at a time and you'll have a great deal of effectiveness in using your knowledge to make your way through life. Try this out and evaluate your results!

References

Fernandes, M. A., Wammes, J. D., & Meade, M. E. (2018). The surprisingly powerful influence of drawing on memory. *Current Directions in Psychological Science, 27*(5), 302–308. https://doi.org/10.1177/0963721418755385

Stanfill, S. (1978). *Classroom practices in teaching classroom English.* Anchorage Community College of the University of Alaska.

CHAPTER 4
DEVOURING THE TEXTBOOK

Jack Cole

"You cannot open a book without learning something."
— Confucius

Textbook Use

Here's one thing to remember: a textbook is like a refrigerator. It has order and organization and can be used accordingly.

When you get up at 3 a.m. and want a snack, it's possible to go to the refrigerator and get one. However, you don't start at the top left and eat everything you find and then eat the next item to the right and then the next and the next and then go to the second shelf. No! You look things over and select what you want, regardless of the shelf it is on.

However, many people treat a textbook like it is a lawn they have to mow. They mow one strip, then turn around and go the other way, mow the second strip, and so on. They repeat the process until the lawn is done. It takes time to get to what's at the end. If that's what you want, look at all the time wasted.

Yes, a textbook or any book, is like a refrigerator, and should be used accordingly.

Look at the parts of books:

Title page
Publication information page
Foreword
Preface
Table of Contents
Chapter 1
Chapter 2
Chapter N
Notes
References
Glossary
Index

Each of these parts serves a purpose. When using a textbook, you should use its structure to get the most out of it. So, "tour the book" before you start "reading." This is a higher-order form of reading, by the way.

Read the title page. Discover who the author happens to be. Read the complete title and subtitle, if any. Perhaps notice the publisher. You would be surprised at the number of students in a typical college course who don't know the names of who wrote or edited the book. This information is important.

It's a favorite question on final exams, by the way. You should know who wrote the book and refer to them as you speak or cite the book. The names of the authors happen to be one of the primary ways that scholars refer to and store information. Get on board with this. Dragons do.

Look at the publication information page. This tells you the edition of the book, when it was published, the publisher and city of publication. It also gives you the ISBN – International Standard Book Number – which uniquely identifies the book. This is used by the U.S. Library of Congress and book vendors. You will need this information when you reference the book, should you be writing a paper. Go ahead and get it early on. A simple cut and paste can do this for you.

The foreword is an introduction to the book, written by a person selected to be knowledgeable about the topic and perhaps an individual of some note. Often, it puts the book into historical context and remarks about various notable aspects of the book – how it was written, how it approaches its topics, the reception it received at the time of prepublication and afterwards, who else has something to say on the topics, and other useful information.

The preface is an introduction to the structure (chapter by chapter) and contents of the book. It is usually written by the author, but sometimes by the publishing editor or some other individual. It is your roadmap to the rest of the book. Here, you'll find important terminology (key words) and ideas, as well as a layout of the progression of information represented in the chapters.

By the time you're done with this, you'll have a good idea of what's in the book – and be prepared to be more selective in your reading, rather than starting at the beginning of chapter one and reading every word until you've found the information you are looking for. I read very few textbooks from beginning to end, unless I want the layout to lead me through the author's thinking, step by step. Remember, a book is like a refrigerator.

The table of contents is the list of chapter titles. You should read through it carefully to see what the book contains and how information is to be presented. You can use it as a jumping off point to information of particular interest or see it as a road map to the information contained in the book. Using it carefully can be a great time saver and make the book have more value to you.

I usually check off chapters in which I have particular interest. For example, if I read a book on Roman emperors, I usually want to find information on Marcus Aurelius first. This helps me "cut to the chase" and find the specific information I want. Other information on Marcus Aurelius can be found by consulting the index. Dragons get "big ideas" this way.

The chapters in a textbook or general nonfiction book tend to have similar structures. This is your key to rapid and effective reading. Chapters contain:

- Opening or Introductory Paragraphs
- Body Paragraphs
- Summary and Concluding Section
- (and sometimes) References or Follow-up Thoughts or Questions or Suggestions for Further Reading

At the very least, you should read the opening and closing sections of the chapter. To gain an overview of chapter contents, you should skim the beginning sentences of each section or paragraph. This will give you a good idea of what's in the chapter before you read it closely (every word, perhaps skipping words you already know) for full comprehension and information.

By the way, if a page has five or more unfamiliar words, you should consult a dictionary, look unfamiliar words up online, or see the glossary at the end of the book. Repeat as necessary, as they say. Read them all or just consult the ones you need. I write notes on the margin of pages – 25% of a book is blank paper, and you may as well use that blank space. I mark and underline important concepts; sometimes I highlight important things.

The notes section explains items in the text. Sometimes this follows the chapter itself, or it may be seen as endnotes at the end of the book, arranged chapter by chapter. If you want to follow ideas out to their end, the notes explain them in greater detail or tell you where to go. Sometimes they are worth reading in their own right, since they often contain author-researched information that did not make it into the book (possibly because it would have disturbed the flow). Some people relish reading the notes.

There was a book in college called the Norton's Anthology of Literature. When we used it in our classes and for writing papers, we jokingly called it the Norton's Anthology of Footnotes! Not only were there often more footnotes on the page than there was original text, but the notes were also often more interesting.

The references at the end of the book are the sources used by the author in crafting the book. It is a useful gauge of how scholarly and completely researched the book happens to be. It gives you an idea of "who" the author knows and where you can go for more background or commentary on the topics in the book. References are formatted according to a standard style. American Psychological Association, Modern Library Association, and Chicago are popular citation styles. When you reference a book, use the format you find or translate it to conform to your own format needs.

The glossary is a list of key words, with definitions to make them more accessible to the reader. I always look at it, but usually find it less than useful when reading the text. However, teachers often use the glossary as a source of questions on quizzes or exams, so you should look through it. Who knows? Many people find it useful. Sometimes you find examples that work for you in understanding what you read.

The index is a listing of key and important words in the text. Names, places, dates, words, ideas, concepts and other important pieces of information are accompanied by a listing of every page on which they appear throughout the book. It is an exceptionally useful tool.

An index is a joint effort between an author and the editors of the book. They mark the words in the chapters that they consider to be important, and software does the work of collating, arranging and paginating where the ideas occur in the text. It is one of the most important parts of a book for a scholar wishing to follow an idea closely throughout the development of the book.

You should have a look before you start reading the book. It could be that the information you seek is in a chapter other than the one you'd expect. This is "word to the wise" information. Take a good look at the index.

There are many ways to read, and you should select the one that meets your needs. Each returns its own particular degree of comprehension, so you get to pick and choose accordingly.

You should also "shift gears" between your mode of reading to suit your needs. Reading at one speed can render you dysfunctional at understanding what you are reading and, literally, put you to sleep. Have you ever fallen asleep while reading? If your reading is taking too long, try one of the methods below.

DEVOURING THE TEXTBOOK

I once had a woman who took 8 hours to read and to report on a textbook chapter of 15 pages. The average time spent by my learners at the time was an hour, maybe a little more (but not much). I got her to speed up by using the methods below. It changed her life.

A few of the modes of reading for information (not necessarily for enjoyment) are:

- Close reading
- Skip reading
- Skimming
- Survey reading
- Sampling
- Targeted reading
- Annotating while reading (or taking notes)
- Hanau© method

Most adept readers use a mix of these when reading. A few comments about each follow:

Close reading means reading every word, thoughtfully. In this mode, you read at little more than the rate of speech and savor the ideas as you go, letting them sink in. Sometimes you "hear them in your head." This is the most intensive way to read.

I think you get the most out of your reading this way. Sometimes, you get so absorbed that you lose track of time. That's not a bad thing. Good creative thinking (think-along-and-beyond-the-text) can occur here. Dragons read closely.

Skip reading means you jump over words you already know, without stopping to pronounce them. You skip words like: *and, or, for, to, is, we,* etc. This gives you the brief view of what's in the text. You can always slow down and read more intensively.

Skimming is like skip reading, except that you speed along until you find something you need to read more closely, slow down, read closely, then speed back up. This is good for finding "nuggets" of information.

Survey reading is a structured reading approach, geared to getting the absolute most out of what you read. It refers to a method pioneered by Ohio State professor Frank Robinson, which he called SQ3R, or Survey, Question, Read, Recite, Review – and it is a great method for mastering text for the long haul or for an exam or quiz. It takes some learning and goes like this:

- First, <u>survey</u> the chapter. Read the titles, first sentences and key/italicized words, noting definitions or boldface type. Do this from the beginning of the chapter to the end.
- Second, create <u>questions</u> to guide your reading. Turn each title or section heading into a question and read to answer it.
- Third, <u>read</u> the chapter section by section. State the answer to each question as you go. This is a good way to take notes, so you can feel free to write your answers down. You'll end up with a great summary of the chapter.
- Fourth, at the end of the chapter, <u>recite</u> – reread your questions and tell yourself the answers from memory if you can. If you cannot, feel free to peek.
- Fifth, <u>review</u> all of your questions and recite their answers at a slightly later time (half an hour will do) to test your retention.

And, as we say, repeat as needed for each chapter. Dragons do.

Sampling is jumping through text, stopping to read what "catches your eye" or interests you. This is the *Reader's Digest* approach to reading and it can be quite rewarding, in many ways.

By the way, I recommend *Reader's Digest* for leisure reading, language and vocabulary development, and the building of general knowledge. It is a great gift for young people and new learners of the English language.

Targeted reading is looking through text for specific information, and then reading it. Chapter structure can help you here. Look through the index and then look at the text. It is often accompanied by highlighting and dog-earing pages, or by taking notes.

Annotating while reading (or taking notes) is a key form of scholarship, with an eye to the future. Often, you take notes to fit into something you're writing or composing. Putting an index into your notes is a good idea here, so that you can re-access ideas later on.

The Hanau© method is a "crash-intensive reading" strategy designed for really dense material – material that puts you to sleep, puts you off, puts you into a stance of non-comprehension. It is a method of analysis-by-synthesis that tears a passage apart so you can understand and master it. It's often called "Statement PIE." (Hanau, 1974).

A friend of mine used this method, and it helped him immensely. This led him to understand that the prose paragraphs in nonfiction writing contained a pattern: a Statement (often called a topic sentence) sentence followed by one or more of three types of sentences: Proof, Information, or Example. Once you identified the purpose of each sentence, you could comprehend the paragraph more completely. This, plus diligently looking up new words, helped my friend earn his Ph.D.

Paragraphs can have the Statement at the beginning, at the end, or in the middle. Just identify it and see what the other sentences do. That being done, the paragraph's meaning will be open to you. Try it when the going gets tough.

Whatever you do, remember that your style of reading determines your comprehension, and it can affect your retention of information. Taking reading notes on the page or in your notebook is always a good idea.

Remember to shift gears as needed. After all, reading is a highly complex process that involves your whole brain (Kweldju, 2015). Remember to stay alert. When your attention flags, take a break. Set a timer and come back. Or take a walk or a nap or get something to eat. Breaks are important, as long as they don't interrupt your work too much. I once had a student who took a break from class for two months, but it didn't help her grade.

Conclusion

Chapter 4 contained a variety of smart approaches for reading and learning from textbooks. For Dragons to devour the textbook, they leverage these skills in order to make the very most of the time they invest in reading. Mastery of even one part of it and using the skills outlined will enhance your capacities as a learner, a worker, and a citizen.

References

Cowan, N. (2001). The magical number 4 in short-term memory: A reconsideration of mental storage capacity. *Behavioral and Brain Sciences, 24*(1), 87-114.

Hanau, L. (1974). *The study game: How to play and win with Statement-Pie*. Barnes & Noble Books.

Kweldju, S. (2015). Neurobiology research findings: How the brain works during reading. *PASAA, 50*, 125-142.

CHAPTER 5
BEFORE YOU GET STARTED ONLINE

Jack Cole

"The human spirit must prevail over technology."
— Albert Einstein

What we know is based on what we learn. As we go through life, what we learn is guided by our questions and interests. It's a good idea to always keep these in mind, since you never know where or when you'll run into useful information, regardless of what you're looking for at the time. If you have a standard way of acquiring new knowledge, you'll save time and be more effective. Using a computer, going online and getting information allows you quick and ready access to information. This is a key to a great deal of learning in our century. It's also important to be alert to the quality or originality of the information. Fresh information originates with human beings. It's good to remember that.

Right Now Questions

What are you looking for right now? Are you looking for questions about a subject you may have? If so, try making a list. Are you looking for information about topics of interest? If so, you can either make a list or you can have a list already in place.

Forever Questions

What are you always interested in learning about? List the topics and questions and set a mental alarm to let you know when you come across some of this information. If you react by gathering the information into your notes established above, you can get back to the task at hand in short order.

For instance, my list might include information about:

Science of Learning
Music
Guitar
History
Famous People
New Orleans
Cajun Culture
Key West
New Books
Weather and Climate
Job Market Trends
New Apps
Philosophy
Physics
Nanotechnology

Before You Go Online

Prepare a strategy for acquiring and storing the information you encounter and for determining whether you need to keep it or not. Having notebooks, memory drives, and cloud storage available is a good way to be well prepared. Prepare your workspace to accommodate these.

<u>Mattering in an Online Classroom</u>

When you participate in online activities, you become like Alice when she is in Wonderland. Falling down the rabbit hole and finding the tiny door the tiny key fits, you find yourself "way too large to fit through into Wonderland." Your challenge becomes that of projecting some yourself through the doorway into what lies beyond. This is important for meeting your learning goals.

In Carroll's story, Alice drinks a liquid that shrinks her to a size that will fit through the door. You aren't so lucky; all you have is the Internet. Fitting yourself through the small avenue that presents you is a real challenge for the foreseeable future.

It would be nice if you could push a button or click or just stand in place and have the computer transport your hologram directly into an image of a real classroom. At your place. Seated at your desk. Standing. Walking around. Able to see everything and everyone. Comfy, yes? Unfortunately, not at this time. Maybe never. It depends on what designers, manufacturers, developers, educators and others, including school boards, principals and others want us to have. That's a complex calculus, and you and I generally aren't involved. Technology expands accordingly to "what can be done" and what's profitable, and that's what's sold and that's all people can buy.

We wait for what comes and deal with what is. We need to orient ourselves and our thinking to our place in time and technology at the time. When you rise in the morning, you get dressed for the day. What you wear depends on the day you expect, and you select your clothing to add to your representation of yourself to the world. Your shirt and jewelry and hair and shoes make a statement, both about who you are and what you think. I often wear my "I Read Books" T-shirt, my "I Read Banned Books" T-shirt, or my "Scars are Tattoos with Better Stories" T-shirt. It depends on my mood and where I'm going.

On days when I teach, either virtually or in a physical classroom, I usually wear a business shirt and tie. The tie provides customization. That ensemble screams "I'm here and ready to work" to my colleagues and students. I have a black and gold school tie, a Silver Surfer tie, a Maryland tie, and Old Bay ties, but I wear them for special occasions. I wear comfortable shoes since I teach and need to be on my feet. Rule number one is "comfortable feet or comfortable seat."

You're going online for class, or for a work meeting, or a social meeting, or business meeting, or to make a speech or presentation. How do you present yourself so that you matter in the way you want to matter? Pretend you're seeing yourself in a mirror. What would you like to see? Dress and compose yourself accordingly.

<u>While Online</u>

In getting ready to go online, you need to consider:

- Your background
- Who are you and how would you like to present that to viewers/listeners?
- How you look and sound
- Try recording yourself and viewing/listening to yourself.
- You may wish to enhance how you look or act
- How your voice will sound
- How you will address online co-learners and colleagues
- One to all

BEFORE YOU GET STARTED ONLINE

- One to a few
- Titles, titles and last names, first names
- How to use the broadcast tools effortlessly
- How to cue yourself as to what to say
- How you will capture information and notes
- How you will plan for follow up and use of the information
- How you plan to communicate with your classmates while meeting
- Raising your hand
- How you will begin to talk
- How to signal that you're done talking
- The timing of the online presence and of your participation
- How to interact with others
- How to signal agreement and disagreement
- Learn and initiate "sign" language
- Respecting formats
- How to discuss
- Running a discussion
- Establishing rapport and communication with the host
- Leveraging your online presence – requesting an audit
- Watching yourself online

<u>Staying Online</u>

Rules of the road. What is the communication channel? Does it stay open? Does it go to sleep and need to be reawakened? Does it close after a period of time?

As you can see, the connection is complex. And this just describes your direct connection with the meeting you attend. You also can use email, platform resources, text, phone and social media. We'll ignore these for now.

Back to the main channel. You have varying degrees of control over each element of the channel. You could conceptualize it as a circle, but in my opinion, circles don't wield as much power in discussions like this. They just look pretty. And because looking pretty begins with you, we should start there.

You → Your Computer →Your Connection →Host System→ Host to Participants → Back to You

You are the communicator here, and you need to know what you look and sound like. Dress for success, whatever that means to you. Your audience will ultimately decide, but you have the first say in the way you put yourself together. Choose your clothes and grooming carefully. You may wish to standardize these fashion statements, or to vary them every time out. That's your choice.

What does your audience see? Your face, your hair, your hands. So what do you do with your face? Your hair is important, so make certain it sends the message you want it to send. Your hands often appear on camera, so pay attention to your hands. These are many things you do for a job interview, and remember that everything is a job interview. Remember that cameras have a mind of their own, so check yourself on your screen.

Your Computer

Your computer is greatly under your control, although cosmic rays, solar flares, power glitches, and gremlins all affect it with maladies.

Many of us have no idea what happens inside our computer – it just works. Until it doesn't. Just as it used to be a point of pride for people to know how their car worked and how to fix it, it became a point of honor for some to follow that idea into cyberspace. And to the extent that you do that, you are better prepared to deal with technology.

But when your computer doesn't do what you need it to do, it is your responsibility to get your computer back on track. One-time events are one-time, but repeating events are a sign of trouble – and computers rarely heal themselves.

It is your job to keep your computer in good shape. Run diagnostics. Make a log note about what goes wrong. Check all plugs and settings. When you get to the point of doing all that you can do, take it to an expert that you trust, or one with a guarantee. Sometimes problems with the screen are due to a software driver needing to be updated. (Easy.) Sometimes it is due to a mechanical or electrical problem. (Needs professional help.)

It's the same with every piece of equipment. Did you ever see a worn keyboard? The worn letters tend to be RSTLNE – the "Wheel of Fortune" letters, most used and often the first to stop working. Fixing one key can be done, but it's likely time for a new keyboard.

A great time to look at your computer is before each semester begins. Upgrading memory is often a good idea. Upgrading software can be critical. Finding out what software you will need to use is essential. For example, last semester we used Blackboard Collaborate and had a woeful experience. Even worse, Collaborate was "optimized" for use with Google Chrome and not with Safari. So, I fought to get Apple users to use Chrome throughout the semester. The ones who were the most resistant got the worst grades since their presentations usually went sideways and that cost them points. To summarize, give your computer a checkup.

You also need to know where you can get a usable backup computer for when yours is in the shop. I hate to say this, but many students use "my computer doesn't work" as an excuse for missing several assignments or classes. To combat this, line up the use of a friend's computer, or know where to go to get online at the university library and computer labs. And never trust your own computer with your only copy of anything. Always use a flash drive to back up important information, even if you have an external backup drive. Don't trust the cloud, whether it's the big ones in the sky or the smaller ones at your university.

Your Connection

Your connection to the Internet is complex, since it involves your computer, Wi-Fi, your internet provider and its system. Mine is fairly unpredictable. Indicators of the strength of this connection seem to rise and fall with time, weather, atmospherics, power fluctuations, network strength, proximity of computer to router, extender strength, and phases of the moon – well, you get the idea.

When asked "What's happening with this?", people give you varying answers (rated by us according to whether or not their advice works) according to their degree of tech savvy. Your problem can be a variable one (most difficult) or continuous (easier to solve). When online with Blackboard Collaborate, there is an indicator of connection strength visible to each user. As moderators, we can see everyone's indicator, and they always vary from excellent to poor. In a few years' time, that won't be a problem, but for now you must treat it as fixable.

Keep a log of when your connection drops. Look for a pattern. When your connection is weak, what happens? Do you get knocked off your connection? Do you have difficulty logging back on? Does rebooting your computer help?

If you are using Wi-Fi, how far are you from the router you are using? Walls, pipes, and distance all have an impact on things. Try moving into the same room as your router. Get your computer close to it and see if that makes a difference.

Try getting an Ethernet cable and cabling directly to the router. Don't forget to go to *settings* and to tell your computer to talk through the cable – that usually means changing your Wi-Fi settings. If that helps, you're ahead of the game. In fact, you could run the cable from the router to your computer where you like to work. If you move back to your original location and the problem resurfaces, you have a big clue as to the problem. If you don't feel like moving the router, get a range extender and tie that to the router and then connect your computer to the range extender.

If you still have no luck, call your Internet provider. Often the tech team there can boost the signal to the router, or they can reset it. You're paying for this, so use the service you can get. Keep a list of help numbers.

You might consider stronger Wi-Fi. I've discovered that most consumer laptops, including my Dell, are underpowered against today's and tomorrow's upgraded Wi-Fi standards and software. I have an Inspiron, which is a "people" computer. Now I'm upgrading to a Dell Latitude which has even more Wi-Fi punch. That will hopefully further reduce my connection problems. Next step after that is a desktop computer, full-sized, with stronger Wi-Fi. If that doesn't work, maybe I'll get a new provider. There's always something to try.

The point here is that a poor connection is your problem to solve, not an instructor's or the host's. Just as having a workable computer is your responsibility, so is the connection where you live and learn.

When it comes to technology, some students have a "victim mentality," which means that they rely on others to maintain their computer's usefulness. Not getting knowledgeable and capable in a big hurry is a big mistake. I call it "willful ignorance."

Contact your university's office of technology. Google your problem. Call a computer store. Talk with your favorite personal tech wizard. Do something to solve your own problem. No one cares or is affected by it more than you. It's a major part of the work ethic that you project, and remember that everything is a job interview.

Host System

The host system is the set of networks, computers and storage devices maintained by the organization you contact to use your class or meeting software. It talks back and forth with you – and with the companies and databases it makes available to you while you're logged in. It assigns you your ID and password. It usually has an arm of its IT department dedicated to maintaining, fixing and improving it – and to providing user services and consulting on demand.

If you see messages about downtime or maintenance when you log on, heed them. Parts – or all – of the system may be nonfunctional. If parts of it malfunction, call or email the help team. Calling is my favorite approach. You learn the names of who's out there to help you, and you quickly learn to differentiate the stars from the duds.

Some host systems are better than others. However, they are complex and need constant attention – and people are always out to hack or to disable them. Watch the system messages it sends to your email and, if you have difficulties, text a friend and see if they're having the same problem. The bigger the host system gets, the higher the probability that there is a problem somewhere. Use protection software.

Get to know your host system. You'll be surprised at what you find. The ones I use have several different options for logging in and using them. If one doesn't work, I can often use another. Also, keep in mind that things usually work better during the day when technology help desks are staffed.

If the host system is down or doesn't work for you, log it. If you have assignments due, contact your professor and try to send them another way. At least you'll be able to demonstrate on-time submission or intent.

Host to Participants

When you are in a virtual class, sometimes the participants don't hear you or see you or react to your request for interactions. This could be a problem with the way the host thinks you're set up to work. If this happens, check your video settings and your audio (there's usually a way to test before enabling these). If you are using an add-on microphone, be sure to test and to make sure it works. Same for an add-on camera. Check every time.

Wireless or plug-in earphones or headsets can provide an extra layer of problems on your end. You are better off keeping things simple. The days of the headphone look are over. They're great for fun or for music, but a bit much for class.

If your classmates have trouble hearing you, try adjusting your microphone volume. If that doesn't work, ask your classmates to adjust their speaker volume. You might ask your instructor to give you a quick lesson on the platform you are using. Instead, you may need to get technical help. Doing so says, "I want to get this mastered." This is a great sign of a strong work ethic. As the Dragon says, "Getting help is a sign of strength."

Back to You

If you are not getting great communication with a meeting, remember that the host system has to send signals to you, and for all the reasons cited above they might not be optimal. Logging off and restarting your browser, and then perhaps your computer, might give you a better experience. Sometimes you can log in using your phone instead.

Follow the same steps for fixing things that we've considered above. Then consider calling for help. Again, this shows a good work ethic.

Organizing to Benefit from Being Online

You should also consider taking care of the items below before you go online. They can help you succeed and to project a good work ethic.

Your background

If you sat in front of yourself (or used a mirror), what would you see? What's the backdrop that your camera will send to your viewers? Is it one that will show you in a good light? Will it allow the lighting to show your best features or will it "drown you out" visually? Many cameras aren't optimized for all skin tones, so you may want to add light to your environment to show you off to a good advantage. You may notice that this can affect your choice of clothing. Clothing that is too light can "wash you out."

Also, what's on display behind you? A bookcase, a flag of some sort, a blank wall, or a big mess? Are there a few things that genuinely express who you are or are there things you wouldn't be proud to show to your grandmother? A ledge with random junk strewn all over it? People use your background to assess you, and this affects the way they determine your credibility. My students who broadcast from bed with their headboard showing behind them certainly sent a message to me and to their classmates. Is that the message you want to send?

If you're not sure about your background, have a Zoom meeting with some friends and critique each other's background visuals.

How you look and sound

Take charge of your presence in a virtual classroom. Either record yourself during a test session and look at that or have a friend critique you. I'd do it myself first. Then you can adjust your mic and camera settings accordingly. Remember, some of this is the way you control your technology. Don't neglect it.

How your voice will sound

Your voice is you. Professional speakers realize that their voice is, in a sense, their career. If you care about your voice and you depend on it a lot, get some coaching or professional training.

Your speech is worth your effort. Neglect it at your peril. If you do, you will rarely know that it's the reason for your lack of success. Many people who have worked to improve their voice can tell you that it matters.

How you will address online co-learners and colleagues

One to one

Many people will tell you how to address them. "Call me Dr. Cole." "Call me Jordan." Alternately, there are rules of address in professional situations, such as school or work. Call people by their titles – Mr., Mrs., Ms. or whatever honorific applies to them, such as Governor, President, and Madame

Chair. Downgrading someone by calling them something more informal than what they deserve or expect simply ends up in downgrading their opinion of you. If someone tells you to address them by a first name or nickname, feel free to do so.

One to all

If you are addressing a group, use "everyone," "friends," "classmates," or "fellow learners." Avoid using the term "guys," unless the group is all male. In the workplace, "colleagues" works well, as does "friends." Do not assume that people want to be addressed as you would. This is especially true with groups of strangers.

One to a few

The rules of address are a little looser when it comes to addressing a smaller number of people. "Team," "you all," "people" all work. Often a group will have a name, and you can use that. The key rule is not to offend. Dragons master this.

How to use the broadcast tools effortlessly

Learn your broadcast tool and practice using it before you present. This is most important. Rehearse all aspects of the platform before the presentation. Don't expect it to get easier to use if you just launch into your presentation. All potential problems will rise up to bite you if you do. Moreover, not being fluent with the tools of the platform is an insult to the audience, just like not bothering to learn the pronunciation of every word in it. Practice your presentation, with timing, at least three times. If something doesn't work well, eliminate it or do it another way.

If you are using a browser with tabs, perhaps open a special tab for videos and switch to it when you need your video to run (you will of course have already opened the video in the tab and put it on hold, preferably with Closed Captioning enabled, which helps if the video feed isn't first rate.) Run your presentation slides from another window, and know how to switch back and forth between them effortlessly.

If your instructor has told you to use a particular program or not to use another, follow that recommendation. I have told my classes to use Chrome because our platform works well with it and seen students use Safari, which does not, and their grades paid the price.

How to cue yourself as to what to say

Make yourself notes, preferably on paper, and place them next to your computer where you can see them by glancing at them. For the most part, look at the camera, but few people will notice if you glance to the left or right to check your notes. Do not put your nose to the desk to see your notes. Wear glasses if you need them.

How you will capture information and notes

Taking notes during an online class is a smart move (Morehead et al., 2019). Keep a notepad by your computer and use it. You may use a grabber like One Note if you are capable of doing it effortlessly while you are presenting. You may also request that attendees use the chat during the presentation. If you see these in real time, you can respond to them.

How you will plan for follow up and use of the information

Remember that some of the information you will gain online is of practical use to you. Note it down and mark it with an asterisk (*) for future reference. During or after the session, note where you might find it useful (for final, for research paper, to tell my friends, for casual conversation, for job interviews, and so on). The Enhanced DaVinci Notetaking System© is ideal for this. You can go to Chapter 3 for more details about how to use this system.

How you plan to communicate with your classmates while meeting

Learn and know how the chat function works. Set up a chat group with your workgroup or friends so that you can "crosstalk" and comment during presentations. Be aware that many online meeting platforms also record the chat sessions, so be careful of what you say. The instructor can also see all chats unless you use a chat program outside the session platform. Remembering this can save you embarrassment and possible loss of reputation.

Raising your hand

There are two basic ways of "raising your hand." Either use the "raise hand" function on your screen or wave your hand at the camera. Sometimes the presenter can tell who wants to speak and sometimes not. Be helpful.

How you will begin to talk

When beginning to speak, remember that there is a lag between your voice starting and the microphone successfully switching on and capturing what you say. Therefore, it is wise to begin your utterances with "This is _____." That will give the microphone time to fire itself up, let folks know who is speaking, and give them time to focus on you as the speaker. It's only polite to do this. If you're important enough to have something to say, you should be important enough to let your colleagues know who is talking. Don't just assume that they'll recognize your voice. In the name of class participation, I track who speaks in my class. If I don't know who's talking, they get no credit. Is that worth it?

How to signal that you're done talking

By the same token, you should signal when you've had your say. Say something final, like "that's all," or "Thank you." That signals the end of what you intend to say. Don't you just love students who go on and on and never let you know they're through and then get upset when you "step on them?" I certainly don't. Do not be one of those people.

The timing of the online presence and of your participation

If you are given a time allotment for your online presentation, honor it. Use a clock. Set a timer. Have a friend send you signals. This shows respect for the audience. People lose track of time when they're talking. Use whatever aids you need to respect the audience. It is a major crime to take other peoples' allotted time. It insults speakers coming after you, and it insults the audience. That's why rehearsal is so important.

How to interact with others

Long ago, pilots would communicate by radio. Only one person could talk at a time. So, pilots ended what they had to say with "over." That let the recipients know that it was their turn to speak.

When interacting with others online, you should do some version of this to let others know that you are done and that it is now their turn. Speak and end with "and you?" If you don't recognize who is speaking, interrupt with "who is this?" If you do it enough, you build a habit of appropriate wait time in the group. Sometimes the instructor will serve the traffic direction role for a discussion, but you often have to fend for yourself in a virtual classroom.

How to signal agreement and disagreement

If you agree with what you're hearing, sometimes there's an "agree" icon to click. Sometimes there's a "disagree" one, too. A savvy speaker will ask an audience to raise hands to indicate agreement or disagreement. Be ready to do this quickly. The lag time includes the time for the speaker to ask, for you to think and respond, and for everyone else to do so, too. Some people are notoriously slow, and in that case, they should abstain from responding, since the speaker may be well into the next point. Holding back like this is a sign of politeness. Stay tuned in and be on top of this.

Learn and initiate "sign" language

There are two kinds of "sign" language. The first consists of waving your hand at the camera. Wave. Thumbs up. Thumbs down. The OK and peace signs. Remember, however, that the thumbs up and the peace sign are considered quite rude in some cultures. You can also show numbers by wiggling the appropriate number of fingers, particularly when rating an idea.

The second type of "sign" language is to actually show a sign to the camera. Timing signs. Yes/No signs. True/False Signs. Letters in answer to multiple-choice questions. There are many ways to do it. Perhaps your host/instructor will facilitate this. Of course, American Sign Language is appropriate when it is understood by all. Using it to a select few in an audience is like whispering and is considered to show bad manners. You wouldn't want to do that.

Respecting formats

If your instructor or boss requests work from you, it may be required in a particular computer format. If so, respect this request and, whatever sort of files your computer produces, your job is to translate them into the required file format.

The major computer programs for professional office work are Microsoft Word, Adobe Acrobat, Excel, and PowerPoint. These produce files with last names (file extensions) .docx, .pdf, .xlsx and .pptx, respectively. These names might change in the future, but they are the mainstays right now. Graphics files may be .pdf, .jpg, .png, and others.

Other computer programs produce files with hundreds of last names, and there is usually a way to translate them to one of the approved file types. If not, you can buy a commercial program to translate files. You should do this if necessary. Often, your university office of technology can help you with this. Your instructor is entitled to receive the way work the way it is specified. Your job is to make that happen.

Moreover, many programs save files to the cloud and allow you to issue an invitation to your instructor to "come and get it." You should not do this due to the fact that it makes extra work and often requires the intended recipient to enter personal data or to sign up for a service to make this possible. This is not a professional or a wise thing to do.

In both cases, you should convert your files to the approved format, save them on your computer, and submit them. Personally, I see so many files that I can't take the time to either convert, translate or fetch files that are difficult to get. I simply lower grades. There have been cases where a usually good course participant has received a D or an F in a course because of not doing this. It says this in my syllabus. You are expected to know how to use your computer appropriately. If you do not, call the tech help desk or better still, take a course. Challenge yourself to become more tech savvy.

How to discuss – and how to dialogue

During online meetings and classes, topics of interest, information and questions are often put up for consideration. There are two basic ways of engaging in this, according to experts like Deborah Tannen (2007) of Georgetown University.

A discussion is a conversation where one person speaks and then another speaks to what the first person said. Often it seems like a ping pong or a tennis match. The first speaker says something, and the second speaker responds with "but…" and says something. The conversation proceeds like this. It is often used as a way to get to a conclusion or a solution to a problem quickly and effectively. This may be so, but this form of conversation may leave many alternatives out. It is useful when a quick solution is needed.

A dialogue is a conversation where speakers build on each other's comments, using the conjunction "and." Understanding is built throughout the conversation. In fact, a final solution or consensus may not be reached, but more factors and ideas get included along the way.

So, if you want to discuss (note the "cuss" root, like percussion, and concussion – "striking"), use "but" and feel free to contradict what you hear. If you want to dialogue, use the word "and" and build upon what you've heard. Both have their place in conversation, and they may be mixed.

Sometimes the moderator of the session will set the tone so that speakers tend to use one or the other mode. Become facile at using both and you'll have greater flexibility in speaking.

What does this have to do with technology? This distinction is important when conversing online, since turn-taking and civility are more difficult when you are not actually in the room with other discussants. Knowing these things helps to facilitate more productive talk.

Establishing rapport and communication

Find out as much as you can about your instructor. Personality, background, training and education, turns of phrase, likes and dislikes, habits and procedures all help you make interaction and communication easier and more effective. This is to your benefit.

Does your instructor like to use email? Chat? Text messages? Phone calls? At what hours? On which days? Are there "office hours" or online office spaces available for your use? How should you set your speaker? Often, instructors are online for several minutes before meetings start. It's smart to log on early and have some talk time with your instructor. This builds rapport and allows you to be known.

I know who to expect will be online when I start class. I come to count on that. We know each other better. Those who maintain silence or "lurk" but do not talk – don't generally do so well. I track speaking and responses to questions. If I still don't know who you are at the end of the semester, there's less "cushion" in your grade or in my opinion of you. That means that you should speak out--especially if you are an introvert.

Being an introvert is great. It often means that you are a deep thinker, but it doesn't help you or the ongoing discussion if you are online. Then it gets read as unwillingness to participate. It's easier for an instructor to deal with "over-talkers" than it is to deal with non-talkers. Whether you talk or not is your choice, but there are the consequences. Make yourself known.

Leveraging your online presence – requesting an audit

Get a friend or two to watch you present and to offer suggestions. You could even get a professional speech trainer, coach or a speech language pathologist to help you. This can be painful, but you can learn a great deal.

Watching yourself online

Play back and watch a recording of a presentation you have made. Today's platforms make that easy since they can record all sessions. Make notes as to what you do and don't like about your presentation style and work to improve it. If you don't, you'll make the same errors every single time. Professional speakers do this as a matter of course.

Conclusion

There is more than meets the eye with virtual learning. We share these tips from the perspective of professors who have seen students soar or sink in our virtual classrooms. We've been learning the strategies for years. Have we mastered them all? No, but we are always ready to learn new ones. With the Dragon Mindset, you stay hungry to learn more, eager to improve yourself. We urge you to do just that. The Dragons say, "Practice, practice, practice," and that's good advice.

References

Gibson, J. J. (1972). *The senses considered as perceptual systems.* George Allen & Unwin.

Morehead, K., Dunlosky, J., Rawson, K. A., Blasiman, R., & Hollis, R. B. (2019). Note-taking habits of 21st century college students: Implications for student learning, memory, and achievement. *Memory, 27*(6), 807-819. doi: 10.1080/09658211.2019.1569694

Nichols, R. M. (1957). Listening is a 10 part skill. *Nation's Business.*

Tannen, D. (2007). *Talking voices: Repetition, dialogue, and imagery in conversational discourse.* Cambridge University Press.

CHAPTER 6
ASKING FOR HELP: PROBLEM SOLVING AND NAVIGATING BUREAUCRACY

Todd Kenreich

"The person who tries to live alone will not succeed as a human being." – Pearl S. Buck

It may seem like the most successful students don't need help from anyone. They sail above us as if they are totally self-sufficient. Well, they're not. The truth is that we all need help now and then. For those with the Dragon Mindset, asking for help is a sign of strength, not weakness. Overachievers know this, and they stay sharply focused on what they can do and when they need help (Micomonaco, & Espinoza, 2022). In this chapter, you'll learn to refine your problem-solving skills and deftly navigate the college bureaucracy.

Finding Your Way through a Maze of Campus Offices

It is easy to get lost on any college campus. Often, the campus map and signs don't help much. Sometimes, all of the buildings look the same. It can be difficult to decipher what is where. The bureaucracy of the university can be difficult to handle. What's the problem? Where is the information that you need? Who has the power to help you solve your problem? How do you contact them?

Remember, of course, that every single person who works at the university is paid to help you. Your tuition helps to pay their salaries. So, you already pay for their help and services—whether you seek their help or not.

Even though this is true, keep in mind that not every university employee views their work this way. Some faculty, staff, and administrators are less focused on the unique needs of students. As a result, some are not interested in helping you. Yet, the savvy student finds a way to leverage the people and resources of the campus to their advantage by building relationships (Felton & Lambert, 2020). What follows are four examples of problem-solving in action.

"Who is the Bursar?"

A sophomore, Alex, receives notice that her window to register for classes is around the corner. She knows which classes she would like to take; however, on the day of her registration, Alex discovers that there is a hold on her account. She can't pick her classes, and she begins to worry that her preferred classes won't be available for long.

Alex asks her roommate what to do. No idea. Then, she texts her mom for advice. Check with your advisor. Next, she emails her academic advisor about the hold. The advisor replies, "Dear Alex, I'm sorry to hear that you're unable to register. I just checked your account, and there is a hold from the bursar's office. You should call or email the office at once."

Alex locates the phone number for the bursar's office and calls it. A recorded message begins, "You have reached the bursar's office. Our menu options have recently changed. Press 1 for hours, press 2 for general information, press 3 for billing questions, press 4 for payment options, and press 5 for the front desk." Alex presses 5 with the hope of reaching a human being.

The front desk staff answers the phone. It turns out that Alex's university won't let students register for classes if they have an unpaid balance for tuition and fees. Now what to do? While talking to the bursar's office, Alex asked if there was a team member who could help her identify why there is an unpaid balance. She later learns that funds from one of her scholarships have not yet been deposited into her account. With this news in hand, as unwelcome as it is, she doesn't give up.

She asks the bursar's office for the contact information of the coordinator of her scholarship. At first, the office staff explain that they do not have contact information because this is a scholarship from an external donor.

Alex, then, asks one last important question, "If you were in my position, what would you do next?"

The staff replies, "We expect this scholarship will credit your account by the close of business tomorrow. Let me check with my boss to see what we can do for you. Hold on a few minutes." To Alex's great surprise, the staff was able to temporarily move other funds to pay her balance while the university waited for the scholarship to be deposited in her account.

Not all rules can be bent in your favor, but being persistent like Alex can make it much more likely that you catch a break here and there.

"Oh No, My Class is Full?"

Sophie, a first-year student, heard from her friends that she should take at least one class with the award-winning Professor Jackson. Her friend explained that Dr. Jackson is brilliant, funny, and kind. He teaches one section of Psychology 101 each semester. As Sophie begins to register for classes, she discovers that Jackson's class is already full. Now what?

One option is to pick another class and move on, but Sophie really wants to learn from a popular professor who is beloved by his students. So, Sophie emails the professor directly to ask if she can be placed on a waitlist for the course. Dr. Jackson replies, "I don't maintain a waitlist, but let's have you come to class on the first day. Remind me that you need to be added to the class, and I'll see what I can do for you." While this is no guarantee, Sophie feels confident that she has made every effort to take Dr. Jackson's class. One the first day of class, Dr. Jackson informs Sophie that his secretary will add her to the course.

Classes with popular professors often fill up quickly during class registration. It makes sense to register as early as possible. Doing some homework ahead of registration is the best way to ensure that you are prepared for picking the right classes. Meet with your advisor well before your class registration window. For most colleges, you'll need your advisor's approval first to register for classes. Also, you'll want to know that you're on the right track with your required courses for your degree. Waiting until everyone else is registering for classes is a recipe for frustration and delays because it is much more likely that your advisor is busy meeting with other students.

"To Drop or Not to Drop Chemistry"

In high school, Blake was a relatively strong student. He arrived at college expecting to sail along by putting in about the same amount of time and effort as before. As a first-year student, Blake studied for his midterms and did well in all classes except for chemistry. Having taken honors chemistry in high school, he felt confident as he began general chemistry in college. However, he earned a D on his chemistry midterm. This was the first D on any test he had ever taken. He began to wonder: *Maybe I'm no good at college-level chemistry? What happened here? Didn't I study enough? What should I do next?*

One option is to quit. Blake could simply withdraw from the class. This would mean that a "W" would be recorded on his transcript. One W is not the end of the world, but a string of W's does raise questions about a student's ability to persist in demanding situations. Before making this decision, he should keep in mind that he will lose money by dropping a class.

In the first few weeks of the semester, most colleges give a pro-rated refund. For example, if Blake decided to drop chemistry in the third week of the semester, he would receive a 50% refund of the tuition for the course. However, Blake is in the seventh week of the semester. At his college, no refunds are issued after the first month of classes. Is it worth it to quit? No, Blake decides. He'll stay in the class.

What are his next steps? First, Blake chooses to stop by his professor's office hours in order to review his midterm and ask about help sessions ahead of the next exam. Blake realizes that he made a few careless mistakes with his chemical equations, and he misunderstood a key concept from the second week of class. In a cumulative course like chemistry, misunderstanding a foundational concept can be costly. But now Blake has re-learned the earlier concept.

Going forward, the professor suggests that Blake attend extra tutoring sessions offered weekly by the chemistry honor society, a campus club. Looking away and blushing, Blake feels too embarrassed to attend tutoring sessions. After all, he took honors chemistry in high school. He never imagined that he would need tutoring—certainly not in chemistry. Sensing Blake's hesitation, the professor reassures him that peer tutoring is designed to help all students and encourages him to attend at least two sessions. To Blake's surprise, the first tutoring session is really helpful, and later he sends a short email to thank his professor for the suggestion.

> "The best advice that I would give to those going to college is to take your education seriously. Stop looking at college like your professors are doing you a favor. If you fail to learn something, then learn from your failure. Use all of the resources on campus and off-campus to figure it out. "
> -Third-Year Student

"But, I Already Know How to Write!"

Kya, a political science major and junior, is taking an upper-level course on the Supreme Court. From the first day of the course, she sensed that her professor had high expectations for her students. The professor found time to share her many accomplishments: law review, federal clerkship, attorney, and pro bono work with immigrants. Kya felt in awe of her professor—mostly inspired and a little intimidated by the professional success of her professor. Kya was eager to prove herself in the course.

The first writing assignment was to prepare a short paper on a landmark Supreme Court case. Much to Kya's dismay, she received a C on her paper with numerous comments from her professor. She was not accustomed to receiving so much feedback. Never had she received so many comments on a paper before this one. So, she decided to meet with the professor during office hours.

As she entered the professor's office, she felt nervous. Kya wanted to impress her professor, but now she felt that her writing was a disappointment to the professor. She took careful notes on additional suggestions that were offered. During the conversation, the professor recommended that Kya visit the writing center for the next assignment. At first, Kya felt defeated and thought to herself *But, I already know how to write.*

Her professor then shared a story about her own writing practices. Writing, she explained, is very hard work. In a distracted world, it can be hard to focus. But, more than that, it is rare that the first draft of writing is perfect. When her professor was a college student, she went to the writing center. Over time, the writing center helped her write more concisely and coherently. In graduate school, her professor joined a writing group that provided support and constructive feedback on the writing process. Kya felt encouraged when she learned that even professors have to work on their writing, and she decided to give the writing center a try.

> "My advice is simple: reach out. It is never too late to ask for help with anything, and it is never too late to ask another question. There are plenty of resources available to help you—no matter what the circumstance."
> -Fourth-Year Student

Conclusion

Keeping a clear, vivid view of your future success in mind can help you persist as you navigate campus resources (McMichael et al., 2022). By design, colleges provide a wide range of services to help students succeed. Remember that your tuition unlocks these powerful and life-changing opportunities. The Dragons say, "Be strategic and leverage these opportunities to your advantage."

References

Felton, P. & Lambert, L. M. (2020). *Relationship-rich education: How human connections drive success in college.* Johns Hopkins University Press.

McMichael, S. L., Bixter, M. T., Okun, M. A., Bunker, C. J., Graudejus, O., Grimm, K. J., & Kwan, V. S. Y. (2022). Is seeing believing? A longitudinal study of vividness of the future and its effects on academic self-efficacy and success in college. *Personality and Social Psychology Bulletin, 48*(3), 478–492.

Micomonaco, J. P., & Espinoza, B. D. (2022). Psychological mind-set and student success: The importance of internal locus of control in students who overachieve. *Journal of College Student Retention: Research, Theory & Practice, 23*(4), 1078–1098.

CHAPTER 7
BUILDING RELATIONSHIPS WITH PROFESSORS AND PEERS

Todd Kenreich

"Choose people who lift you up." –Michelle Obama

With the Dragon Mindset, you now have tools to deftly navigate the Information Environment and even the campus bureaucracy. For this chapter, we highlight the importance of building relationships with others. This is essential not only for your academic success, but also for your overall well-being. Your mental, emotional, physical, and spiritual health is tied in large part to the quality of your relationships (Miller, 2021).

When we asked several hundred college students to offer advice for those just beginning college, they consistently explained the vital importance of setting aside time to meet new people, make friends, and seek mentors. We begin with steps to get to know your professors, and then we offer tips for making friends in college.

Faculty Office Hours

Faculty are required to be available to students for a few dedicated hours each week. Often these hours are posted online and within academic buildings. Find out when the hours are and go. Give notice before you stop by. A short email will do. Don't overthink this; just go to office hours.

Introduce yourself and ask for a few minutes to talk about a topic from class, an upcoming assignment, or better yet, ask them how they got interested in their field. Asking someone to talk about themselves can open up the whole conversation. Keep in mind that some faculty hold office hours virtually instead of in person. If that's the case, be sure to arrive early to the virtual platform (Zoom, WebEx, Google Meet, Microsoft Teams) so that no technology issues work against you. Building a relationship with a professor makes you feel more invested in your learning.

Emailing Faculty

Here are a few tips for how to email your professor. First, remember that an email message is more formal than a text. Be sure to include a few key words in the subject line, and then start with a greeting such as "Dear Professor X," and notice the capitalization and punctuation used here.

Second, less is more. In general, an email message should be no more than a paragraph. If, for example, you are sick and will miss class, consider these messages:

> Subject line: [empty]
>
> hey prof so did i miss anything on monday? i wasn't in class
>
> Josh

> Subject line: Sophia Jackson's absence for 9/28
>
> Dear Professor X,
>
> I wanted to let you know that I will be absent from tomorrow's class. I have a fever and sore throat. I will be sure to check with a classmate for any missed notes and keep up with this week's readings. I will bring a doctor's note when I return. If there is anything else I should do to stay up to date with classwork, please let me know.
>
> Thanks,
>
> Sophia Jackson
> 2pm Monday/Wednesday section 5 of HIST 101

How do the messages represent Josh and Sophia? The latter message above works far better than the first message that we've received again and again over the years. Sophia demonstrates that she is responsible and ready to make up her work. Including her full name and date of absence in the subject line helps the professor immediately understand the point of her message. It is clear that Sophia took time to proofread her message. She also signed the message with her full name and listed the corresponding course, section, and time. This is important because most professors teach more than one course each semester, and this helps them identify the right student in the right course, right away.

With Josh's message, on the other hand, notice the empty subject line, the overly informal greeting, and the lack of capitalization and punctuation. Without a subject line, his message fails to quickly convey its purpose. Remember that professors take pride in their mastery of the language, and they expect you to do the same.

How does this message represent Josh? Little care and effort were put into this message that was sent after the absence. Asking if he missed anything is sure to irritate the professor. It is as if Josh is hoping that the professor will casually reply "No, you didn't miss anything."

How did the first message represent Sophia? She demonstrates that she is responsible and ready to make up her work. In the end, Josh is a decent person who forgot that an email message to the professor needs a more formal tone than that of a text to a friend.

Keep in mind that professors get dozens of messages every day in their inbox, so don't expect an immediate response - especially to any message sent moments before class, during class, or in the middle of the night. However, feel free to follow up politely via email or in person if you don't receive a reply within a day or two.

Letters of Recommendation

In four years of college, you'll take more than three dozen classes with as many professors. But, in the end you only need two or three professors to write you a letter of recommendation. So, be strategic and choose professors who can put in a good word for you.

Take it from us, professors need some time to write you a good letter. Whenever a student asks us for a letter, usually our first questions are: 1) what are you applying for? 2) what's the deadline to submit the letter? 3) what's the submission format? and 4) could you email your resume? For the best letters of recommendation, professors need to know you and your professional goals.

The best time to ask for a letter is **at least three weeks** before your deadline. In general, the earlier, the better. Do your homework ahead of time so that you can answer these questions with precision. And what if the professor says no? Don't worry about it. Just move on. Reach out to another professor.

Mentor

A mentor. Just the word alone sounds intimidating, doesn't it? Seeking a mentor is humbling because it's a reminder that you don't know everything. But that's okay. You don't know everything. You're in college to learn from others. Seeking out someone who really knows more than you do is always a smart idea. This may be a faculty member. Review the college website to learn more about the unique areas of expertise of various faculty. What have they written? What projects or grants are they working on now? Do your homework to learn more about the faculty. Take a class with a professor who may be a good candidate as a mentor. What if your favorite professor doesn't really want to be a mentor to you? Move on. Find someone else who does.

Keep in mind professors have a lot on their plate. They are busy with many projects. It's not that professors don't want to mentor students. They often do make time for polite and persistent students. So, be polite. Be persistent. Seek a faculty mentor.

Not all mentors need to be professors. One of the best ways to get ahead in college is to find classmates who actually are one or more semesters ahead of you. These students can become informal mentors who share inside knowledge about which professors to take, which ones to avoid, which classes are a breeze, and which ones aren't.

Building relationships with professors is extremely important. Also important is making sure that you have friends. You do not need me to tell you the benefits of being friends with people. But, you may need help meeting people.

To meet people, you'll need to start by putting yourself out there. We all have different levels of energy and interest in going to social events. When you join a new campus community, you need to eat right and get enough sleep so that you have the energy to show up, be present, and be engaged in campus life.

Keep the Door Open

If you choose to live on campus, be sure to make the most of the experience. After all, when else in your life will you live with a bunch of people your age? Consider how to include roommates and neighbors in your activities. Announce when you plan to go for lunch at the dining hall. If it's lunchtime, there is a good chance that someone else is ready to walk with you to the dining hall. What if you invited others to join you for lunch, but no one texts you back? Move on. Go to lunch on your own.

The most important time to keep your door open - or at least ajar - is the first few days after you move in. If your door is closed, you're sending messages like "Leave me alone" or "I'm away." Acting like you are inaccessible and above everyone won't help others want to reach out to you. Make yourself available by keeping your door open. Allow yourself to be on the radar of others. Many acquaintances begin in the first week. Don't put a bunch of pressure on yourself, but remember to be open to talking to others you haven't met yet.

Get a Job

Work a part-time job for the university. No matter what your job, you'll begin to feel more connected to the campus community. In most jobs, you'll meet people and make new friends. You'll discover more about the ins and outs of the campus. What's fun to do. Where to go. Where to eat. Insider knowledge of a community. You'll make connections with people who may be able to help you find another more interesting job on or even off campus.

Usually, the student ambassador is one of the better paying student jobs on campus. Can you walk backwards and talk to people? Well, you should apply to work in the admissions office and lead campus tours for prospective students and their families. It's another line for your resume. However modest, it brings a paycheck.

Get Involved

There may be a temptation to be successful by putting all of your energy into your classwork. While your classes and grades are important, there is more to life on campus. Small colleges offer dozens of student clubs and activities, and larger universities offer hundreds. Continue with an interest from high school, or better yet, try something new. Join the intramural ultimate frisbee team or the climate action club. Find the joy that comes from meeting new people with a common interest.

If you're not sure where to start, look for a student activities fair at the beginning of the academic year. This event is sure to offer table after table of clubs and activities that give you a taste of what's available.

What if there is no student club for your life-long love of film or cycling? Contact an officer in the student government association and ask how to create your own club. After all, each club starts with an idea from one student. Why not pitch your idea for a new club? Getting involved is a powerful way to build relationships with your peers, learn new skills, and have fun along the way. What's more, being highly involved in extracurricular activities and campus organizations improves the odds that you'll graduate on time and feel better prepared for life after college (Seymour & Lopez, 2015).

Get the Name Right

Meeting new people means that you'll encounter new names. Some names will be familiar, but others will take some time to learn and remember. How do you feel when someone mispronounces your name or calls you by the wrong name altogether? It's not the end of the world, but it does signal a distance between people. If you expect people to pronounce your name correctly, then you need to invest the time and effort to learn how to pronounce the names of others. One trick is to add any new name to a note on your phone. Write the name phonetically and practice saying it out loud to yourself. Quickly, you'll master all of the names and impress your friends.

Remove the Earbuds and Put Down the Phone

No one wants to feel socially awkward, but sometimes that's how we feel with others—especially when meeting new people. Some people can walk into any social situation with ease, and if that sounds like you, then you have our permission to go ahead and skip to the next chapter. For the rest of us, it is quite common to feel a bit uncomfortable with new people in new settings. As a result, there may be a temptation to use your earbuds and phone as a way to avoid or escape some social situations. Resist the temptation.

Remove your earbuds and put away your phone so that you can lean into the present moment. Practice your ability to start a conversation with someone new. Be ready to actively listen and make warm eye contact. Small talk can have big consequences. It can be the gateway to a new friendship.

Small talk often starts with everyday observations. On the perfect day, you can note, "It's a great day to be outside." You are stating the obvious, and that's okay. It opens the door for someone to agree with you. Or you can commiserate with others. When out in the heat, you can say, "I can't believe how hot it is today."

If talking about the weather sounds like something your grandparents do, you're right. But, the weather - however beautiful or severe - is always there for you to observe and use as a hook to talk with someone else. When standing in line, empathize with others. "I wish this line was moving faster." "I'd like to sit down." These honest statements can be a small beginning of a larger conversation that moves deeper to what's your major and where's your hometown.

Another approach is to offer a small compliment. A little kindness goes a long way. You can say a nice word about what someone says or does or wears. Mark Twain once said that he could live for a whole month on just one compliment. You get the idea.

> "Be kind, honest, and hard-working. It'll pay off. Make friends. Everyone's on this journey together. Call your parents often. Wake up early enough to get breakfast at the dining hall; it makes all the difference. Befriend a worker there. Don't spill Mountain Dew on your laptop. Save your work. Ask for help. Thank your professors. Give grace to the ones who don't understand you. Go to the cheesy events on campus and don't be afraid to show some school spirit. You'll have more fun." -Fourth-Year Student

Conclusion

Smile, be brave, and strike up a conversation with someone new. It could be the start of a life-changing friendship. With the Dragon Mindset, make time to engage in events and activities on campus so that you can begin to feel a greater sense of belonging and connection with those with you on this four-year journey.

References

Miller, L. (2021). *The awakened brain: The new science of spirituality and our quest for an inspired life*. Random House.

Seymour, S., & Lopez, S. (2015). Big six college experiences linked to life preparedness. https://news.gallup.com/poll/182306/big-six-college-experiences-linked-life-preparedness.aspx

Further Reading

Amy Cuddy, *Presence*

> Cuddy emphasizes how posture and body language play a powerful role in cultivating a natural presence where you are anchored in your strengths.

Keith Ferrazzi, *Never Eat Alone*

> Ferrazzi offers a range of practical strategies to build your professional network, and he suggests that it is important to break bread with others.

Don Gabor, *How to Start a Conversation and Make Friends*

> By helping you identify your conversation style, Gabor explains how to strike up a good conversation in any setting.

CHAPTER 8
GETTING READY FOR WHAT'S NEXT

Jack Cole

"Whatever you think you can do or believe you can do, begin it. Action has magic, grace, and power in it." – Goethe

"Next" is a relative term. This chapter outlines a few ideas and explains how you might apply them to craft your future. First we'll look at the big idea and then at the pieces and then we'll put them back together.

The Big Idea

We can manage and control our path through life to some extent. This is because we are sentient. We can look ahead and behind and plan a course of action to create the future we want to achieve. Unless we are people of extraordinary talent, ability, and luck, we need to be masters of ourselves and to take charge of ourselves.

This bears some repetition: You are now in charge of your own learning. You are the manager. You are the boss. You are the planner. You are the guide. What you learn is your business, in every way. All components of your Information Environment (I.E.) are tools for you to use: your mind, your mental/emotional strategies, your habits and practices, school (in whatever forms it may take), teachers, books, computers, printed/written/heard information everywhere, all information everywhere, other people, rocks, trees, stars, and birds. Everything is a tool that you can use to learn from in order to build your world, experience and future. No one else can do it for you, although many people can help.

The old paradigm (the way things were) is that you were a vessel to be filled with knowledge, and that our society and its people were the agents for doing that. Not anymore. The paradigm has been flipped – you are the one in control, and you need to seize control so that your learning benefits you and so that you can craft the world in which you live and your vital role in it. The people who allow themselves to become passive vessels become tools for others to use. You don't want that. Resolve right now to put yourself in charge and to progressively learn what that means and how to do it.

> "College is a time for you to start trusting yourself and trusting what you know. It is a time to find your voice while listening to others as much as you can. This will help you take that next big step in life after college." -Third-Year Student

The Pieces of the Big Idea

In Chapter Two, we explained that we live in an Information Environment (Gibson, 1972). Everything in this environment may be converted to information by the perceptual systems of the organization encountering it. This environment represents the perceived – therefore, real – experience for the organism and may be both inhabited and manipulated by that organism. In a very real sense, we make our reality by participating in it.

We may consider the possibilities represented by the Information Environment and may act upon it to craft new and desirable realities. In other words, we create our present and future experiences through our efforts and reactions to what we perceive. If we want to be a dancer, we conceive of ourselves through the assumed lens of "dancer" and interact with our environment by dancing. So it is with all other things.

Of course, we may encounter various degrees of success in doing this, but the principle holds nonetheless. My nervous system, musculature and balance may make me a lousy dancer – but I can be a dancer nonetheless. The world is full of people who have made a living by being lousy at something. Go figure.

Our Information Environments are virtually limitless. While there may be an absolute limit on their extent, for all practical purposes, these environments are limitless. Their features are rendered into information through the actions of our perceptual systems and, as information, form the building blocks we use to construct our past, present and futures. As Claude Shannon (1948) and others established in the mid-20th century, a bit of information is the amount of information needed to reduce uncertainty by half. That is a rough rule, but it is the basis of cybernetics, the computer revolution, and logic (Boolean and otherwise). So, how will a coin toss turn out? Heads or tails (or, rarely, a stand-on-edge result, which everyone discounts, particularly if the coin is well-filed on the edge) define the possible outcomes.

Now there really is no such thing as one simple scientific measure of learning, but we can assess learning by comparing prior learning states to post learning ones. We must design the "package" or measure by which we assess whether learning takes place, but it can be done. That's called "assessment," and it's a fairly messy business, but schools and teachers sometimes get pretty good at it. We can also conduct this operation on ourselves and find it more satisfactory, although sometimes it can go far astray of its initial purposes.

As sentient beings, we conceive desires for future states and turn them into plans. These are routines of behavior designed to let us achieve specific outcomes in life, or in our interactions with our Information Environment. We may spend a lifetime pursuing a plan – or a moment or two – and several plans may be in play simultaneously.

People are complex combinations of plans. Once you know their plans, you can craft a pretty good idea of what they will do. Marketing is built upon this set of assumptions. It is a powerful tool for dealing with individuals and groups.

The more conscious you are of your desires and your plans, the more you can refine them to produce the results you want to achieve. There are well-focused plans, and there are more diffuse and unfocused ones. The former are usually more effective.

The more clearly you can see ahead, the better able you are to craft your future and the path to get there. It's pretty simple. Moreover, interaction with Information Environments works best for personal development when it is unfettered – unconstrained and free of all negative or outside influences that attempt to guide its path in ways that are not free for the individual.

GETTING READY FOR WHAT'S NEXT

> "Don't wait until senior year to go to the career center. Stop by right after you arrive as a freshman. Take the career inventory right away. Be sure to use every resource that your college provides because they can help you in the long term. Always reach out to professors, ask for recommendations and seek help when you need it. Never be afraid to ask for help. Professors love to see a student putting forth effort with a desire to do better!" -Fourth-Year Student

How This Works in Practice

As you stand where you are now, there are several vistas ahead, depending on your overarching purposes in life. Depending what purposes you decide to pursue, the ideas and strategies in this book apply in different ways. Some of these purposes include graduate school, internship, online learning, full-time employment, gig-based employment, personal development, friendships, organizations, writing, creative expression, new skills acquisition, networking, publishing, business opportunities, and even retirement.

More Schooling

If your purpose is to continue (and someday finish) school, there is a traditional and highly useful set of tools for you to use. You will refine, change and extend these to complement your learning as information technologies continue to evolve, and with them, your I.E.

Graduate School

Undertaking graduate school means that you have joined an area of professional work and committed yourself to playing an active role in it. Graduate study will allow you to teach yourself the key concepts, practices, procedures, lore and commonly held ideas pertinent to your field of work. The tools you use to acquire this knowledge are of higher order than the ones used for your basic undergraduate study and link together more effectively to provide immediate and continuous guidance for your actions.

A Master's degree program leads you into the profession as a functioning member. A Doctoral degree program enables you to conduct the sort of research that makes you the developer of new concepts, ideas, procedures and policies affecting your professional colleagues and establishes you as a thought leader in your field. Your "name" becomes associated with your ideas and the things you espouse.

Internship

An internship in a field of work allows you to teach yourself how the work is done by actually doing it. Valuable tools for this sort of learning include good time management, learning through on-the-job training, journaling daily experiences, and improving listening skills. These tools should become second nature. Dragons master this.

Online Learning

We will all be doing online learning, for "class," for the job, and in the wild, for the rest of our lives. It is best that we get used to it – and get as good as possible at it. A journal for learning about learning – and about what we learn – is pretty essential; this can be electronic or on paper. We need to keep track of the themes of our learning and to prompt ourselves to be sensitive to the locations and sources of possible nuggets of knowledge. It is also valuable to index our findings so that we can re-track them and refer to them as needed. It goes without saying that passwords should be tracked. Also, "tips, tricks, n' traps" should be held for later use.

Employment, Full-Time

This is where you ply the trade/craft you have chosen for your professional work. Here, records and journal entries are important for legal and solid work practices, address books serve you over time in several different jobs (and serve as the solid base of your network, which predicts and documents your effective reach in the world of work), and daily routines or practices serve you well in setting both self- and others' expectations for your work style and habits.

These things set others' definition of your persona as a person of high work ethics. Are you dependable? Available? Responsive? It is imperative that you set up a set of files that serve your information storage and retrieval well and with as little error as possible – and which are either encrypted or otherwise safe from tampering. It is also useful to maintain a set of your information databases at an off-site location, in case a surprise job disruption (yours) occurs, as often happens at various points during career experiences.

Employment, Gig-Based

As we meander into the second quarter of the 21st century, "gigs" are becoming more and more common for those of us in the workforce. A "gig" is a temporary task for which we are employed temporarily. Without getting into the pros and cons of gigs, we can probably agree that "piecework," or "gigs," have a number of characteristics in common that require the shoring up of our individual learning regimes:

- Record keeping, accounting and billing
- Contact information and contact management (keep the pipeline loaded)
- Active networking (who can supply the part, piece or information/text needed for the project?)
- Data harvesting and storage

- Staying current with conditions (market, societal, legislative, regulatory)
- Competitors, collaborators, compadres (allies and coworkers)
- Markets and contacts
- Resources and sources
- Life management/calendar
- Long-term goals
- Finding new passions
- Managing your brand
- Plans for the future, immediate, intermediate, long-term
- Skill maintenance and improvement (what's the next skill needed? Data analytics? Tagalog? Crochet?)
- Trend analysis and financial projection
- Health and habits

Often, it pays to maintain a loose association and ongoing communication with a group of allies who co-refer, look out for each other and identify upcoming opportunities. Truly successful "lone wolves" are few and far between.

Personal Development

Personal development is most important in life. It is rarely seen as a legitimate arena for learning and hardly ever considered in the context of the learning tools that can facilitate its advancement. Yet personal development is widely regarded as a worthy enterprise for individuals. Why are the tools useful for its acceleration not widely addressed?

What do I want to do when I'm doing what I want? This is a tough question for many people, but it is an existential question. It is a question regarding fulfillment and life's passion. And very few people ever get there. Yet if it's important to you, how do you learn your way there? How do you find out and then instantiate yourself into your life's passion? What tools can you use to get there – or at least to find and smooth the way? Here are a few tools that you might find useful along the way:

- Journal/diary focused on your search for your life's passion
- Contact list (used continually) of individuals who can serve as dragons, advisors, counsels or sounding boards
- Open social media accounts for exploring these issues
- Excursion schedule for exploring opportunities (travel, museums, trade/craft shows, finding clusters of like-minded people practicing interesting pursuits, clubs, organizations, social groups)

Friends and Acquaintances

You should use this lens as an add-on to your situational awareness at all times. You never know when lightning will strike!

Join a Group with a Purpose

If you find a group whose purpose suits you, you might consider joining it for a while. You might find that its members' interests and activities are ones you enjoy. If this is so, add citations of them to your daily journal and see where they lead you. It could be that the group is organized to support and to feed the workers of a professional area of organizations whose future prospects you find enjoyable and enticing. Feel free to pursue this for a while – or until you discover another area that suits your interests better, and then pursue that. Don't just jump around at random or take this lightly, but realize that your path may be taking you in the direction of what you may find to be a valuable lifelong pursuit. Remember – you are in charge!

Writing

Many of us write as part of our earning a living. Teachers write. Managers write. Supervisors write. Workers in various lines of work write. Reports, requests, requisitions and other things – all professional writing. Some of us write nonfiction descriptions, plans, directions and procedural manuals. Some of us even write stories, scripts, treatments for dramatic presentations, plays or fictional literature (and get paid for it!). Some of us are copywriters (although AI is beginning to crowd this field; still, AI-users will still be in demand, we think).

All this work is information-intensive, and writers should be collectors of facts and information and sources. They should document what they do in a journal and find ways of storing parts and pieces of their writing for future retrieval and use. The standard advice of writers to would-be writers is "write, write, write." This means that planning days with set-aside times for writing is important, so a writer's calendar of planning work is critical to success, particularly on those days when writing seems like the least-likely thing one wants to do.

Moreover, many of us believe that re-writing is the essence of good writing, that recrafting is the most important part of crafting good writing, and that the first draft is rarely the finished one. That's why all writing deserves to have a version number. This keeps a writer from overwriting a decent piece of writing with a less decent one in the name of speed. Every version deserves its own number. Some software tracks this for you; some does not.

In any case, assigning versions by date or sequential number is important, and so is tracking it in your daily journal. If you are a copywriter, perhaps the organization's copy production environment will do this for you. Even though it is often cumbersome, it is worth suffering through it to gain the benefit of good version control. This is not trivial.

Creative Expression

Expressing ideas, feelings, intuitions or prescriptions for the future is what many of us see as being our main function in life. Whether we are artists, composers, creators or craftspeople, we live to project our take on things to the people and institutions around us. Our use of information and the I.E. are the most important parts of what we do, and the creations we form from the I.E. or our own formulations of it become the futures we and our fellow humans inhabit. Many of us are not traditional users of information, but various elements of information tools help us to progress and prosper through our increasingly creative ways of interacting with the world: making a living, planning for the future, developing new projects and bringing them to fruition. We may use some of the more structured tools to help with this: record-keeping, time management, creative ideation. We may be aggressive in our relationships and travels in search of the new or the leading edge of thinking in areas of interest. As craftspeople, we should learn to increasingly respect and refine our tools.

New Skills Acquisition

Every so often, we embark on a quest to acquire or to try new skills and ideas. This is an excellent time to hone and to perfect the use of our information tools, adapted to the new I.E.s which we explore. It is important to consider "What tools will I potentially find useful?" and to select those which you feel have the greatest chance for serving you well.

New ways of gathering information may make sense, as well as new modes of storing it. New ways of processing it in terms of utility – perhaps group processes or modified Delphi (group brainstorming) or the use of consultants may prove useful. It is possible that you may find structured and scheduled revisiting of information to be refreshing from time to time, as well as changes of location for yourself or for your research. Many people find even temporary locations useful for finding new inspiration or ideas; this has been useful for creative people throughout history. You may find it so, as well. Travel is good for this!

Expect new skills to be rough at first, and to become more refined through practice and use. Expect plateauing to occur, and make sure that you persist through it – or move onto other skills and return to a skill later to see if it has been refined with time. Expect and search for surprises.

<u>Networking</u>

Associating with people is a good way to grow your I.E. and keeping track of them in your journal/notes or in a database are excellent ways of keeping information regarding them. Remember, each individual has their own I.E., and as individuals link with individuals, these I.E.s multiply each other, not merely add. Floating questions of interest, even ones beginning "who do you know that…" is an excellent way to use these contacts to mutual benefit. Remember, you have to give to get, and you should go first and keep this up as a practice throughout life, and it will pay you back handsomely.

> "Invest in yourself from day one of college. Build a strong professional network that can help you become your best self." –Second-Year Student

You can craft a network around specific purposes, or you may construct a non-specific, mutual help network – or both. The more people you know and with whom you interact, the better. In many fields of endeavor, the size of your network is an indicator of your worth. Law, medicine, real estate, sales, politics and other fields find that their members gain potency directly in terms of the size of their networks. Why not begin documenting your network now?

<u>Sales and Marketing</u>

This is a real arena for using software for success. Prospecting, finding potential customers, involving them in a sales process and converting them into clients or ongoing customers is a set of processes often best mediated by software and planning strategies of various kinds. Most companies – and individual practitioners – find customers best through systematic and ever-changing processes. It is best to master one and then extend it through others, always being sure that you move your information/network/database from one system to another.

If you are a professional in these areas, it is nearly certain that you will change employers, products and processes and fields of endeavor from time to time, and you do not want to be caught flat-footed with your network of associates, friends and customers cut off from contact with you. Many employers require you to sign non-disclosure agreements as a condition of employment, and many of these have real teeth – on the other hand, a friend is a friend and an acquaintance is an acquaintance and there is a lot of gray in this, so keeping a list of contacts, friends and acquaintances out of the clutches of the company that employs you is an excellent idea. If your company has spent time and money developing your network, they have a claim on it, but if you have invested your time and life investing in the same, so do you. And this process of separation is one of the things that keeps industries vibrant and growing. But you should use apps that allow you to download contact and other information into a handy format.

Many apps have built-in reminder features, which assure that you stay in touch with your network and its members. This is well worth using. The literature of sales is replete with stories about salespeople in traditional department stores who made a good living by merely making callbacks to former customers on an ongoing basis (some of them even used a notecard system).

New Directions

Every so often, some of us like to strike out in new directions. Perhaps we have seen an area we would like to explore, or just want to move and try a new place to live and work. In these cases, it is wise to keep good notes that we can use in resettling and becoming comfortable in our new areas of endeavor. In many cases, our networks have ideas about this and sometimes they even have actionable information for you, too. In today's increasingly linked global I.E., distances have shrunk, and peoples' experiences have expanded exponentially. Being in a new situation no longer means letting go of what one already has – it's often merely one big step in a different direction, while holding onto the old gives one a sense of balance and useful perspective.

But the world is a whole lot smaller now, and this can be useful to us as we set out to explore new things. Sometimes the other side of the world seems more like home than things do around the corner from where we currently live. We may as well make this work for us. I know that I feel at home wherever I go.

Family Business

A family business is a special thing. Certainly, being a member of the family has its benefits. Just as certainly, it has its drawbacks. No matter who you are, the I.E. tool of journaling helps you keep your finger on the pulse of how things are going. When things go well, you need to stay prepared for a downturn, or for it not going well. When things do not go well, perhaps you need to be prepared to take a break from time to time.

You need to be prepared to care for the welfare of the family as well as for the welfare of the business – and these may be two different things, intertwined or not. Good record-keeping and good network maintenance are critical to your long-term well-being. Outward-looking strategies may help you stay committed to your family business – or they may help you ascertain when it's a good idea to take leave of it.

Publishing

Getting your ideas down on paper so that others can see them – and getting them into peoples' hands to read them – that's publishing. Doing this in an organized fashion can be facilitated by software and hardware. Keeping a list of publishing companies contacted is essential. And their responses should be tracked. For larger efforts, it is useful to track your expenditures of time and money. And, of course, publishing can take many forms, so that your use of your I.E. and its networks is both useful and work tracking.

Online Business

Online business is information-intensive. Online sales presence both tracks itself and requires you to be at least as vigilant of its numbers and how it is faring as is a brick-and-mortar retail store. Budgets, billing and accounts payable – as well as government and tax reports – need to be handled. All of the usual components of sales, marketing and distribution need to be managed. People who have transferred businesses from brick- and-mortar ones to ones entirely online have found themselves no less busy! In fact, the business-end of the business may be the primary consciousness of the proprietor, and not the items or ideas being sold! Often, it is useful to engage a partner who likes the business-end of business so that you can focus on what is being sold. Then, all you need to give your primary attention to is the inventory, input, and trends! Again, you will find journaling to be a most useful daily enterprise!

Retirement

We know what you're thinking. Retirement? Isn't it too early to think about this? Retirement used to mean that one stopped working at 65 years old and lived on savings or the income from investments, a pension, or a retirement plan. In the 21st century, however, it seems to mean something different. You're likely to live to your 90s. Retirement means finding a purpose or pastime that supports forward movement in personal development or fulfillment. Otherwise, it seems to be a recipe for slow degeneration and passing out of this life. You need to have something positive to pursue, whether it be art, reading, different work, civic engagement, working with neighbors, community activities, exercise or other interests.

In general, retirement from the workforce means having the freedom to pursue the things you want to pursue, and to find fulfillment in them. This sounds a lot like switching gears, but since our society has less use of your "productive" capabilities, you can now turn your energy into things that produce fulfillment for yourself. One thing that seems to be useful may be leaving a trail – or a record of what you've learned that others may find useful. If one of your descendants finds it so, you have done a worthwhile thing.

OODA Loop (Situational Awareness)

OODA is an acronym for the components of the situational awareness loop. This is known and practiced in the military, and it is essential for good health (staying alive) in many different sorts of situations. It is a key tool for dealing with the Information Environment, particularly for the individual looking for useful information.

OODA stands for:

<u>Observe</u> (look/perceive your surroundings)
<u>Orient</u> (focus on elements of information that call for your attention)
<u>Decide</u> (make a decision where this information merits a response)
<u>Act</u> (take an action in response to the information)

Both purposeful and random exploration of the Information Environment have their merits, and you may choose to use either at various times. Random exploration turns up information that is unconstrained by former biases, and this may be most valuable, indeed, in formulating a future course of action. It is, however, often less effective and productive than its counterpart and more costly in terms of time and effort. Often, one is better off by leaving one's random buffers on at all times, picking up on serendipitous information as it occurs.

Purposeful, or focused, exploration looks at the Information Environment to discover expected and looked-for information that is predicted by certain needs. For instance, when driving down the road in a hungry condition, one looks for road signs that announce restaurants or fast-food places rather than ones that announce retail stores or auto services. Even though food may often be had at a retail store or auto service establishment, it is generally far more effective and efficient to make one's turn-off-the-road choices be those which directly promise food.

Even though this seems like a simplistic example, it also applies to significantly more important features of looking-out that affect us in life – search for jobs, partners or spouses, investments, courses of action and other significant elements related to successful living.

In the end, you may be better off using purposeful exploration of the I.E., augmented by a little habitual random searching. The choice is yours, after all. However, if you start searching without a plan, you rarely find what you want. But, in every case, you are better implementing the OODA loop as you work with your information environments.

There Are Many Information Environments, For Your Information

You have a large Information Environment, which contains all the others. Every realm of information in which you are interested (whether you know it or not) relates to every other information environment. Consider your I.E. as a system of information with subsystems – a system of systems, all interconnected between them.

Moreover, all humans on the planet have their own I.E., itself a system of systems. All of them overlap to some degree, which is why we can talk about them using shared languages (also information systems). And all of the information may be considered as building blocks, with which you develop and build your own I.E., or reality, past, present and future. Talk to people.

GETTING READY FOR WHAT'S NEXT

<u>You Build Your Reality Using the Information You Have (or Don't Have)</u>

Our realities are combinations of the information we have (or desire) and the realities inherent in the I.E. we confront or inhabit. These realities are flexible and malleable – we can craft them as we go.

It is possible to change your reality by making appropriate assumptions about the world and by making use of relevant bits of information. We assemble this information and mold our assumptions as they go.

What follows is a set of guides for working with information in the various enterprises described above, and outlined below:

- More Schooling
- Graduate School
- Internship
- Online Learning
- Employment, Full-Time
- Employment, Gig-Based
- Writing
- Creative Expression
- Sales and Marketing
- Online Business

The Charts

Use the charts in the Appendix as guidance for your selection and use of the various tools for working with information. Feel free to adapt and modify them as you go, and to keep your options open.

> "If you don't know what to do next, don't feel the need to rush and find that thing. Believe it or not, what you need to do is slow down and take some time to talk to others who are doing interesting things that you'd love to do. They'll help you, but you have to ask them." -Third-Year Student

Conclusion

Getting ready for what's next is truly up to you. The Dragons know this, and they are always thinking ahead. They take the time to reflect on their short and long-term priorities. Each day they take those small steps along the path to success. Be a Dragon and soar to new heights of success in your life.

References

Shannon, C. (1948). A mathematical theory of communication. *The Bell System Technical Journal, 48*, 379-423, 623-656.

EPILOGUE

"To be yourself in a world that is constantly trying to make you something else is the greatest accomplishment."
- Ralph Waldo Emerson

So, what's your major? You'll hear this again and again from friends and family. This question is a shortcut that some people use to label you, to measure you. In the end, you must rise above what everyone else wants you to be. You need to be you.

With the Dragon Mindset, you can tackle the challenges big and small that lie before you in college. But, you are more than a student, and there's much more to life than college. As a human being on this planet, you must take up the greatest question: how to live a good life.

Notice that we didn't ask the question as: how to be happy. It isn't that we don't want you to be happy. We do. But we've found that the pursuit of happiness alone rarely leads in the right direction. It will be that still, small voice inside you that helps you find your purpose. Give yourself a few quiet moments each

EPILOGUE

day to breathe, reflect, and listen for this voice. Pay close attention to what makes you feel alive, what makes your heart leap. As you find your purpose, so too you'll find the joy of living.

APPENDIX

The following charts contain information useful to readers interested in several fields. Look through these, select the topic of greatest interest, and apply these ideas to build your future. With the Dragon Mindset, you'll be ready for what's next.

More Schooling

Strategy	Use	Tips, Tricks, n' Traps	Connections	Comments
Notetaking	Capturing information and reviewing it for tests	Use the DaVinci Notetaking system from Chapter 3	This will build a big picture of your learning Use color to spice it up and to make it more memorable	Leonardo DaVinci used a similar system to build his ideas
Listening	This is the primary systematic strategy for gaining information in a classroom setting	It is, arguably, your most important learning strategy	Good listening skills serve you well in all walks of life	
Time Management	Use the Calendar system from Chapter 1	This can keep you from missing deadlines and doing shoddy work	It is work mastering this – the system is the key to good project management, for yourself and groups	
Memory Enhancement	Building a good memory for names and facts can help you stand out from the crowd	Memory improvement is easy and worth doing – it is also enjoyable and life-enhancing	The Memory Book by Jerry Lucas and Harry Lorayne is well worth reading	

APPENDIX

Strategy	Use	Tips, Tricks, n' Traps	Connections	Comments
Textbook Use	Using a textbook well is a primary method of mastering information	This is usually replaced by word by word reading, which is a great way to destroy comprehension and retention Mindless highlighting also works to destroy comprehension and retention	Take a good "Speed Reading" course to build skills in this area Perhaps take a good course in reading comprehension to develop skills at doing this	
Using Information	Information "in the wild" has similar characteristics to textbook information Learn how to read textbook information well and transfer those skills to differently-formatted information	Watch to learn the structures, forms, guideposts and highlights of information; see its form and function together and you will comprehend better	Make the study of information into a lifelong practice Take notes on the information structures you discover	

LEARN LIKE A DRAGON

Strategy	Use	Tips, Tricks, n' Traps	Connections	Comments
Presenting	Well-formatted presentations both inform and convince your audience of the ideas and points you want them to acquire	Spend significant time in mastering this art form of communication Modern tools such as PowerPoint and others allow you to master the modern art of effective communication	Rehearse and practice your "hallmark" presentations This will pay off handsomely Always put a conclusion at the end of your presentation and set out to "sell" your audience on "buying" your viewpoint or doing what you suggest that they do	Watch presenters to see who is good and who is not Make and keep a list of your favorite presenters and give each a grade Watch presenters from a broad spectrum of sources
Questioning	Expanding knowledge and ideas	Ask WIFM questions: what's in it for me? Ask WIFU questions: what's in it for you? Ask open-ended questions		Results go in notes, memory, dialogue and later work

APPENDIX

Graduate School

Strategy	Use	Tips, Tricks, n' Traps	Connections	Comments
Notes	Make these a record of your acquisition of useful ideas, procedures	Identify key ideas in your field and their practical applications		Build a pyramid with 101-type concepts at the base and loftier ideas near the top
Conference attendance	Attend major presentations and speeches Get to know publishers and their representatives	Collect ideas and free samples of commercially-available products	Add new acquaintances to ongoing networking database Include conference attendance in your resume	Refresh these acquaintances from time to time
Networking	Meet as many of your classmates / colleagues as possible and note their interests / strengths	Collect and use email addresses to maintain contact		Perhaps assemble a panel of acquaintances to present at a future conference
Listening	Work to listen for key details, which make important differences	Develop specific icons to identity these as key terms for later review	Prepare for exams by focusing on key terms	Depending on your program, start a study group to prep for exams

LEARN LIKE A DRAGON

Strategy	Use	Tips, Tricks, n' Traps	Connections	Comments
Certification	Take practice tests and learn from results	Develop test-taking skills, especially pacing and item-skipping Visually-coded notecards, electronic or paper, can be very helpful with difficult-to-recall items	Plan for periodic review to maintain high level of recall	Prompt for recall testing at strategic times
Library	Assemble a personal library of significant reference books Begin a lifelong bibliography of memorable sources for future work	An ongoing bibliography prepares you for later professional writing and your master's thesis	Think about topics about which you'd like to write as you take your basic and advanced courses Sketch out and write an article or two	
Planning	Work to select an institution at which to pursue doctoral study Work to identify funding sources for advanced study	Meet with advisors and mentors to identify valuable avenues of future development Develop ideas about areas of specialization and interest	Peruse professional publications to identify locations and organizations where you would like to work Consider travel abroad for professional development	Cultivate friends from other countries and dialogue with them about opportunities in their locations

APPENDIX

Strategy	Use	Tips, Tricks, n' Traps	Connections	Comments
Information Environment	Draw a comprehensive picture of the I.E. for your professional area of interest	Use paper / pencil or program like Inspiration or Mind Manager to allow continual addition to this	Keep your OODA loop operational to keep expanding your view of pertinent information	Stay alert to opportunities and query mentors and advisors regarding new areas of interest (Asking "What's New?" is always a good idea)

LEARN LIKE A DRAGON

Doctoral Study

Strategy	Use	Tips, Tricks, n' Traps	Connections	Comments
Notes / Journal	This is the story of your developing interests and the repository of your ideas as they develop	Keyword and indexing ideas helps you with ongoing and future writing and speaking	Feel free to refer back to other notes you have taken in your academic journey	Often, these are sources for others looking at the development of your ideas
Listening	Learning to listen for the message behind the message; often nuance tells you more than the words that are spoken	Accurate listening is the hallmark of an effective professional	Look at the results of your listening over time and see if you can discern any improvement If not, return to the listening protocols in Chapter 2 and work to make needed improvements	Good listening often separates the valued professional from the pack of "just so" people
Information Storage	Set up a system for maintaining the integrity and retrievability of the information you amass over time	Using a standard format (APA, Chicago, MLA) for your citations will greatly enhance your ability to write fluently and well	Always spell check and grammar check your writing and presentation slides Always reread them to yourself for phrasing and cogency	There is no such thing as writing – only rewriting

APPENDIX

Strategy	Use	Tips, Tricks, n' Traps	Connections	Comments
Information Security	Always backup your data	From time to time, buy and use an external hard drive to preserve your data	Protect your information at all costs Keep paper and electronic copies of important things Copyright (©) the information to which you want to retain rights	
Conference Presentations	Transform your interests into conference presentations Learn to make good ones, even if you need to pay for some coaching	Get to know "gatekeepers" for the conferences at several professional organizations Join professional organizations in your area of interest – many have special rates for students, and you qualify Volunteer for your professional organization – local, regional, national – and begin the process of becoming well-known	Get and carry business cards (name, affiliation, phone number, email address and so on) Change these as needed, since they're remarkably inexpensive	Building your reputation is in great part your responsibility

Strategy	Use	Tips, Tricks, n' Traps	Connections	Comments
Writing	Write papers and articles about your interests Someday, you will be able to combine these articles into books centered on your interests	Establish a council of advisors to look at, critique and comment on your writing and use this council over time to help you improve	Keep comments you receive regarding your writing Pay special attention to comments which you find unsettling	This may be the quickest way for professionals to improve their writing If you are not a professional writer with a professional editor, it may be your only means of improvement
Networking	Endeavor to craft a circle of friends and acquaintances with interests similar to yours	Again, a database designation in your filing system can ensure that you stay in touch with these people	Depending on your degree of activity, stay in touch with these people at least biweekly	Practice giving and receiving help since interchange with groups like these can yield the highest payoff for you For many people, it is the highest form of professional discourse

APPENDIX

Internship

Strategy	Use	Tips, Tricks, n' Traps	Connections	Comments
Daily Journal	Tracks learning in your internship in detail	Make use of a daily entry for best effect Keyword ongoing issues and interests Annotate key people for future reference	Add people and other items to your database	This may be your best source for future work information and a good way to show growth
Listening	This is noted by others and can be used by you for quickest progress in your work	"How am I doing?" is a good question for you to ask your reporting manager at least once a week	Track your progress here and focus on any needs you uncover	
Pocket notebook	Carry a small (2"x 3") spiral notebook at all times and write in it frequently	Use this to track on directions you receive and their resolution Date and time everything Refer to it frequently	Transfer important information to your larger journal and list of action items	Time spent working with this notebook and other notes is time well spent

Strategy	Use	Tips, Tricks, n' Traps	Connections	Comments
Work Ethic	Project this with timeliness, presence and verbal willingness to undertake any task	Not only does the squeaky wheel get the grease, but the involved intern often gets preferential treatment	Do enough of this to make your presence known, but not so much that you are perceived to be a pest	You may need to self-promote beyond the strict confines of your current job assignment

APPENDIX

Online Learning

Strategy	Use	Tips, Tricks, n' Traps	Connections	Comments
Taking Notes	Write down what you want to remember	Use the DaVinci system outlined in Chapter 3 You can hit print screen for data coming in over the computer, and then save it into a data file In the main, handwriting the information you want to retain is superior for retention and nuance; it is also easier to draw pictures on paper than to use the computer to do things freehand	You should have a notebook for technical things (passwords, keystroke combinations, macros, commands, file structures and such) and another one for information Keeping these by the keyboard on the side of your writing hand is a good idea Over time, you can build a storehouse of good notebooks for reference	Not everyone likes doing this, but keeping notes and storing them is your best bet for building a storehouse of information over the course of your lifetime and is a great habit to have

LEARN LIKE A DRAGON

Strategy	Use	Tips, Tricks, n' Traps	Connections	Comments
Listening and Attention	Pay attention to the screens and to the sounds that accompany them Focus and maintain close attention to grab the most and best information you can	Do not let "screen blindness" afflict you – look at the entire screen to catch all of the icons and actionable "buttons" that can unlock program functions or you "Map" each screen so that you know all of the possibilities it offers you	Do the same with text – look at every feature of written information and listen carefully for nuances hidden in sound and speech	When you are distracted, you lose information When you notice that you are distracted, just redirect your attention to the information Make this a habit and your listening / attention will improve exponentially
Storing Information	Set up a file system for information you trap	Every so often, print a picture of the file structure you are using Every so often, back up all of your information	Information storage schemes become obsolete from time to time Be sure to store old information into new formats to avoid losing it Even paper copies of things become illegible given enough time (toner is only electrostatically attached to paper and falls off given enough time)	Copyrighting or publishing information can ensure its longevity

APPENDIX

Strategy	Use	Tips, Tricks, n' Traps	Connections	Comments
The Cloud	Offsite storage is always vulnerable to data loss, no matter how many times you back up the data	You should always have at least one (preferably two) copies of your data Cloud-based data storage is vulnerable to many forms of denial of service and restoring compromised data is always risky	You really should not need to worry about this, but when you lose data, you've been told	Perhaps the world's best English poet, playwright and author wasn't William Shakespeare – but what happened to the other one? We'll never know
Other Strategies	Capturing, understanding and using information may be done in a bewilderingly complex number of ways		Always ask yourself "Am I using the best mental tools for this job?" Always try out a couple of tools You may see better results	Make a list of your favorite tools Keep track of who uses your less-favorite tools, and involve them in your projects to gain different and valuable other perspectives

Employment, Full-Time

Strategy	Use	Tips, Tricks, n' Traps	Connections	Comments
Journal / Log / Notes	Keep track of happenings on the job Often this is a legal requirement for professional work	Make a copy and keep it at home	These notes have real value, so treat them lovingly	Often these are used to decide legal disputes
2 ½ x 3-inch spiral notebook	Carry this around and write down information to remember	Copy and paste relevant notes to your Journal / Log / Notes Always be prepared to write things down	Use this to write "reminder" notes – "remember to …" and "this reminds me of …" You will be able to make more useful connections at work	This will enhance your reputation as a "tie-breaker" decision maker It will also enhance your work ethic
Listening and Attention	As ever, these are critical for tracking accurately on events and challenges	Ask yourself regularly (perhaps Fridays) "How's my listening / attention? Have things improved?"	Good listeners are generally considered to be good conversationalists, and it costs you little effort	As they say, "You've got two ears and one mouth. Use them in that proportion."

APPENDIX

Strategy	Use	Tips, Tricks, n' Traps	Connections	Comments
Memory	Use notes to jog your memory Learn and practice mnemonics – memory strategies	Very few people cultivate their memories Using visual and auditory memory techniques gives you advantages in the workplace	Since memory is editorial in nature, cultivating yours to be as accurate as possible gives you read advantages in many situations	Since drawings enhance memories, make doodles, diagrams, pictures and other drawings of information whenever possible In fact, colorizing notes is a very useful, enjoyable and rewarding habit
Mental Tools	Learn and use as many of these as possible (see separate chapter) for the best possible professional outcomes for your work	Keep a "toolbox" section in your notes to give you ready access to strategies that work well for you	Share this practice with direct reports, mentees, trainees and interns	The correctly-selected mental tool can produce superior work results in many cases

Employment, Gig-Based

Strategy	Use	Tips, Tricks, n' Traps	Connections	Comments
Notes/ Journal	Keeping track of daily and upcoming events can keep you organized	Make this a daily habit. Even short notes to yourself can assist with avoiding disaster	Use these notes in conjunction with your other information systems	"Making a note to yourself" is advice from the best advisor you have – yourself
Small notebook	Carry this around and use it frequently	Be sure to put your name and "reward if found" on it in a prominent position	Lay this out beside your big journal	This can save you a lot of grief. Don't forget to note collection calls
Record keeping, accounting, billing and collections	Small business software is very useful here, as well as for payroll	Get this settled and set up before you begin your business operations. Have a savvy consultant on hand for help with this	This is the financial backbone of your business. Learn it well	In addition to under-capitalization, errors here are the most dangerous you can make for your business

APPENDIX

Strategy	Use	Tips, Tricks, n' Traps	Connections	Comments
Active Networking	Contact management software is a godsend Set it up as you conceptualize your business	Make this a lifelong practice Back your data files up on a schedule	You can use this to reconstruct your business in case of a disaster	Do not neglect this Remember your benefactors at holidays, birthdays, special dates They'll remember and respond to you better
Data Harvesting and Storage	Collect new data whenever possible	Preserve data in your personal/ business library	Use this for predicting trends, opportunities and competitor moves	Failure to look ahead is failure to plan Failure to plan is a plan for failure
Staying Current	Use online sources, services and free and paid subscriptions to stay aware of what's happening in your markets	Always ask friends, suppliers, colleagues and competitors "What's New?" This can keep you aware of upcoming events you'll want to know about	Read newspapers, magazines, and reports to spot trends and opportunities Watch media to spot opportunities Attend trade shows to spot trends and to identify opportunities	Again, keep your eyes peeled to find opportunities and to forestall dangerous surprises

LEARN LIKE A DRAGON

Strategy	Use	Tips, Tricks, n' Traps	Connections	Comments
Markets and Contracts	Watch trade sources and publications to see what business is being transacted Read local contract announcements to identify opportunities	Begin an informal networking group to keep each other aware of events and opportunities	Try to work at least a year ahead on keeping your pipeline loaded Good business is continuous business, particularly when gigging	Consider having sales or marketing staff to keep their eyes on upcoming opportunities
Resources and Sources	Watch your supply and sourcing orders to ensure that your supply chain is intact Use your receivables software functions to track and to predict this – notes concerning "temporary" shortages can predict immediate headaches	Always have plans B and C available in case supplies for key products/services run out Work with a whiteboard that projects business a year or two out Have lunch with colleagues to discuss current and future market conditions	Put these activities on your calendar and do not neglect them	Work out resource sharing arrangements with other businesses
Life Management / Calendar	Have succession and life insurance plans in place to protect your business	Establish a relationship with a good insurance agency near you	Evaluate and revise arrangements at least once a year	

APPENDIX

Strategy	Use	Tips, Tricks, n' Traps	Connections	Comments
Long-Term Goals	Most businesses operate in a 5-year window However, looking ahead is key to long-term success Finances often drive long-term planning, particularly where expansion is forced by needs to service debt	Establish good relationships with 2-3 lenders from different organizations and build a track record of loans and lines of credit	Avoid under capitalization and loan default at all costs – bankruptcy generally follows	Work to establish long term investments and funds that may be liquidated for emergencies
Finding New Passions	Journal/Notes is the place to identify opportunities for new horizons or expansion without overextending yourself	Don't forget research-enhanced vacations to look for new ideas, particularly when things are going well	If you combine family vacations with research, do not neglect your family or you risk losing it	
Managing Your Brand	Advertise and promote your brand with a well-scheduled set of activities that speak to your audience(s)	Use your calendar for this Don't neglect local events such as trade shows, fairs, festivals and celebration	Promote your business through advertising support for local activities Sponsor sports teams and civic events	Engage in the life of your locale and you will build support there

Strategy	Use	Tips, Tricks, n' Traps	Connections	Comments
Trend Analysis and Financial Projection	Learn to use Excel or other tools in order to track and to project trends and future status of events	Mastery of a good spreadsheet or project management software package is essential for successful business management	Having a staff member do this keeps you at a high level and "out of the weeds" so that you can see trends more clearly	Attend presentations of "trends" in various markets that are offered by various relevant business organizations
Health and Habits	This ought to come first Take care of yourself	Self-maintenance is more important than equipment maintenance	Pay attention to what family and friends tell you	Daily exercise, a balanced diet, and meditation are key to good health

APPENDIX

Writing

Strategy	Use	Tips, Tricks, n' Traps	Connections	Comments
Journal/ Notes	Keep track of daily progress and events	Do this at a specific time each day, particularly on writing days		Good primary source for people looking at your work
Word Processing Software	Essential to your success	Master all of its features		You should be able to export forms compatible with your publisher
Indexing Software	Special purpose software for tagging and pagination	Follow publisher's advice on selection and use	Export format is a consideration here	Some software used to do this, but these features have tended to disappear
Publisher Contacts	Your most important database	Get to know these people well. Research them as you go		
Contracts	Mediate your relationships with publishers	Always keep paper copies of these as well as electronic ones	Compare them. You'll learn a lot	

Strategy	Use	Tips, Tricks, n' Traps	Connections	Comments
Library	Organize sources and library in general	You do not need to use a number system to organize them, but they do need to be accessible to you Keeping book reviews gives you an extra dimension of knowledgeability		Electronic filing systems for e-books are now critical to maintain Don't lose sources you'll need for later
Bibliography	APA, Chicago, MLA – there are literally thousands of stylesheets Pick one that meets your needs and stick with it	There is software that formats sources for you automatically	Keep a lifetime bibliography and it will reward you	

APPENDIX

Creative Expression

Strategy	Use	Tips, Tricks, n' Traps	Connections	Comments
Journal/ Notes	Keep track of where you are, what you are doing, where you are going	Use this to document your activities	This can serve to coordinate all of your activities	Artists' notebooks serve often as the source for inspiration
Business Software	Simple, powerful, useful software for managing your business is available for free	Master this well and it can keep you out of financial, business and tax difficulties		
Spreadsheet	Spreadsheet software can ease the task of staying in touch with clients, potential client or others	Keep this updated frequently so it doesn't get out of hand	Potentially this is your best business resource	
Library	Keep a list/photos of your work, dates, income so that you can document and plan	Use this feature of your I.E. to build a catalog of your work		

Sales and Marketing

Strategy	Use	Tips, Tricks, n' Traps	Connections	Comments
Logbook	Track sales calls and results	Software such as SalesForce may suit you well It automates many features such as callbacks, ticklers, info about clients Be sure that you can get your data out of these packages when you need to bring them elsewhere	This software can save you many hours or days of recordkeeping and thus boost your income	Choosing which software to use is an important decision Don't rush it
Traveling Notes	Organized calendar and workbook can streamline and facilitate your success	It is worth taking a course in how to use these tools	Several companies offer both the tools and the training to go with them Taking these courses and using these tools is often a tax-deductible expense	Again, explore these carefully in order to select one that is useful for you
Investment Software	If you're doing well, you'll need to take care of your own wealth-building and retirement systems	Shop around to several investment firms; this can be a full-time job, but it's worth it	Take this seriously; usually, you're in charge and you need to take care of yourself	

APPENDIX

Online Business

Strategy	Use	Tips, Tricks, n' Traps	Connections	Comments
Online Platform	Usually looking like a website, this can be anything from a bare-bones "here it is and here's how to buy it" website to an extensive replacement for a bricks-and-mortar store	Start simple and build out as you go so that you keep everything in place as you make improvements Keep the "look and feel" similar so as to not put off good current customers	Be certain that the "back end" (the money-making section) works properly at every step, or you may find yourself making ruinous refunds to irate and departing customers	Make regular use of comment sections and of the ability of your customers to leave reviews
A good camera or way to take/post pictures	Merchandise or photos of happy customers are key selling tools for your products / services	Rotate these in and out on a relatively frequent basis; be sure to get written releases for images you use	Keep an image of your business in your mind as you develop it so that you don't end up with glaring discontinuities	
Back End	Have good business software available to run the nuts-and-bolts parts of your business	Be certain that you can export your data to other formats, particularly .csv or Excel-enabled formats	Master and use this software diligently – it is your business	
Business Knowledge	Keep this as current as you can, even if it costs you money	Always be prepared to invest in yourself and your skills	Again, continual self-audit of your skills and needs is a big help	

ACKNOWLEDGMENTS

The genesis of this book was a conversation between Jack and Todd about our students. We noticed elements of what we now call the Dragon Mindset in some students, and we wanted to write more about how the Dragon Mindset could empower all students to be successful in college and beyond. We would like to thank our students for the many lessons they've taught us over the years. We appreciate those students who shared insightful reflections about their use of the Dragon Mindset as well as those who shared samples of time management and notetaking. We also would like to thank Gift Idama, a graduate student at Towson University, for his support with our review of research. We know that his future is bright.

We are most grateful for the steady guidance of Wallace Ting at SchoolRubric from the earliest stages of the book. His vision, enthusiasm, and support helped us bring the book to fruition. In multiple meetings, Wallace was gracious with his time as he patiently fielded our questions. Robert Thornell shared valuable suggestions at the very beginning of our writing process. Richard Siegel carefully read multiple drafts and offered

ACKNOWLEDGMENTS

many helpful suggestions that improved the coherence of the book. Fred Shamlian kindly helped us edit several images in the book. In addition, we would like to thank Casey Kenreich for his smart design of the book cover. We are eager to see where his artistic talents take him.

Finally, Jack would like to thank his wife, Lynn, and children Jack IV and Meredith for their love and support as well as for the joy of being a grandfather to Vienna, Odessa, and Adelaide.

Todd is grateful to his wife, Amy, kids Casey, Clara, and Marianne, and his parents Ron and Beth, for their love and encouragement.

ABOUT THE AUTHORS

Jack N. Cole received his Ph.D. in reading education from The University of Maryland and worked as a counselor at the Reading and Study Skills Lab. He has taught at Johns Hopkins University, University of Maryland, Howard University, and Towson University. He has also taught at community colleges and high schools as well as worked in government and private organizations. He was a Reading Supervisor and President of the Maryland Chapter of the International Literacy Association. His interest in learning strategies began in 1960. Married with two grown children, he now lives in West Pittston, Pennsylvania.

Todd Kenreich is Professor of Secondary and Middle School Education at Towson University. He earned a Ph.D. in social studies and global education from The Ohio State University. He was named a U.S. Fulbright Scholar in Japan. Currently, he teaches courses in global issues for teachers, education policy, and professional ethics. His work has been published in journals such as *Theory and Research in Social Education* and the *Journal of Geography*. He also co-directs the Maryland Geographic Alliance, an education network that promotes global understanding through geographic literacy.

Made in the USA
Middletown, DE
28 July 2024